Women, Police and Security:

Reforming the Afghan National Police

Women, Police and Security:
Reforming the Afghan National Police

Melissa Jardine, PhD

2022

© Global Law Enforcement and Public Health Association,
309 George Street, Doncaster, Victoria 3108 Australia

Cover: Photo of street art in Kabul taken
by Melissa Jardine in March 2021

ISBN: 978-1-78324-254-2 (paperback)
ISBN: 978-1-78324-255-9 (ebook)

Contents

List of Figures

Foreword

As the first anniversary of the Taliban's return to power approaches in August 2022, many people are reflecting on the role of the international community in Afghanistan over the last 20 years. This new book provides insights into efforts by the international community to increase women's participation in the male-dominated security sector. Drawing on both face-to-face and online interviews, and other previously unpublished data, Melissa Jardine, PhD. provides in-depth insights into why – despite considerable investment – there was relatively little success in implementing gender-sensitive reforms. Her research identifies how overall international police assistance was often detrimental to women-focused reforms, and that a lack of understanding of the Afghan context resulted in interventions that did not meet the needs of women who were recruited into the Afghan National Police.

Melissa Jardine, PhD. travelled to Afghanistan during the COVID19 pandemic to undertake the research in March 2021. The book consists of the report she prepared for the United Nations which was unpublished due to the advance of the Taliban. The findings are now being revealed for the first time to provide a record of gender-sensitive reforms within the Afghan National Police, and to serve as useful lessons for reforms in other contexts. Crucial guidance is offered in relation to the importance of South-to-South sharing of knowledge and practice and prioritising localised input into approaches funded or led by the international community – who are typically from the Global North.

The book will be useful for academics and practitioners with an interest in police reform and gender-responsive changes for police institutions, especially in the Global South, but also for people in 'developed' countries who are working towards increasing diversity among police to better understand the diversity of needs and aspirations among women with different ethnic, cultural or religious backgrounds.

Preface

In the twenty years of international state-building efforts since the 2001 fall of the Taliban, women's employment in Afghanistan's security sector saw limited progress despite significant financial investment in technical support and training efforts. In early 2021, women still comprised a mere 2.6 per cent or approximately 4,075 women of a total 157,000 workforce of the ANP.[1]

There is a multifaceted environment in Afghanistan with characteristics that interact uniquely to constrain women's participation in the male-dominated security sector, such as: armed conflict, terrorism, organised crime and corruption, among others. Notwithstanding this environment of insecurity, some approaches to women's inclusion in policing were guided by strategies that were more suited to the conditions of the donor states and the places from where consultants – such as myself – were drawn from, rather than being suitable for the realities of and the cultural constructions of gender in Afghanistan.

Decades of research on women in policing in other traditional and Islamic societies would have provided crucial insights for advancing women's participation in policing in Afghanistan, despite its specific

---

[1] 157,000 is used here, however, it is likely to be significantly lower due to attrition and recent reports place it at about 130,000 in 2021; Gender and Human Rights Technical Working Group, Afghanistan (unpublished, 2021).

security challenges.[2] This includes a focus on gender equity and gendered models of policing as a potential pathway to gender equality and an acknowledgement that this is dependent on broader social and political influences. Gender-responsive policing reform does not exist in a vacuum, and ethnic, religious and security issues were not given due regard in the typically rigid and hierarchical policing structures and policies. This meant that policies were developed in Kabul with little nuance as to how they should or could be applied in a way that considered the extent of variation across different provinces.

The overall police reform strategy in Afghanistan under-invested in civilianised and community-oriented policing. Consequently, the necessary foundations on which gender-responsive reforms could gain traction were peripheral, rather than core activities, and thus, under-developed. This disconnect meant that the considerable investment in recruiting, training and deploying women as police officers was undermined. Therefore, while individuals and smaller programs worked to enhance women's roles in policing, their viability was affected by the wider lack of attention on community-level engagement.

This book comprises my assessment of efforts to advance women's meaningful participation in the Afghan National Police for UN Women. In March 2021, I travelled to Kabul to undertake an assessment, and by May 2021, I was advised that final report would not be published due to the deteriorating security environment: there was little likelihood the findings would be able to be implemented in the short- to medium-term. When the Taliban entered Kabul on the 15th

---

2 Natarajan, "Women Police in a Traditional Society: Test of a Western Model of Integration", *International Journal of Comparative Sociology*, *42*, 1–2 (2001); Natarajan, *Women Police in a Changing Society: Back Door to Equality* (Aldershot, UK: Ashgate, 2008); Strobl, "Progressive or Neo-Traditional? Policewomen in Gulf Cooperation Council (GCC) Countries", *Feminist Formations* 22, 3 (2010); Strobl, "Towards a 'Women-Oriented' Approach to Post-Conflict Policing: Interpreting National Experience(s) and Intergovernmental Aspirations", *International Journal for Crime, Justice and Social Democracy* 9, 1 (2020), *https://doi.org/10.1163/156851801300171760*.

of August 2021, it was clear the findings and associated recommendations were no longer relevant.

I received permission from UN Women Afghanistan to publicly share my research in 2022. The research included previously unpublished data and both critique and endorsement of some approaches which may provide useful insights for others interested in gender-responsive police reform. I have made minimal changes to the text of the main body of the research. The key findings of the research are outlined below.

KEY FINDINGS

The initial nature of international police assistance in Afghanistan was detrimental to advancing the women, peace and security (WPS) agenda, exhibiting several critical shortcomings:

- **Prioritisation of short-term security gains** through proxy forces over human security;
- **Lack of coordination** among the various actors providing assistance; and
- **Export of norms and practices** that better matched the conditions of women and policing than those prevailing in the recipient state.

Regarding the role of women within the ANP, the key takeaways were:

- **Women are in greater proportions among non-commissioned officer ranks (**75.77%),[3] perform 'searching' functions (26%) and work in Kabul province and the Ministry of Interior Affairs headquarters (48%).[4]

---

[3] Gender and Human Rights (2021).
[4] UNDP, *Afghanistan National Policewomen Census Survey* (2018), 4, 8, 17–18.

- Taken as a whole, **women police in Afghanistan expressed a preference to work in gendered roles**; i.a., roles focused on clerical work, helping other women, raising awareness on women's rights and pursuing justice for female victims and vulnerable groups.

- The most frequently cited **barriers to a safe working environment** are security (37%) and behaviours towards women (22%).[5] Separate bathrooms and equipment are rated lower at 12 and 11 per cent, respectively.[6]

- **Retaining women in the ANP is reported as a major problem**, yet there is an absence of accurate data on attrition among women staff that could inform mitigation strategies.

- **Peer networks for women police are underfunded and unevenly coordinated**, with additional challenges in relation to ethnic divisions whereby women may be inclined to establish networks according to ethnic lines, rather than gender.

- **Women police experience significant harassment, sexual violence and discrimination** at work, which often goes unpunished due to a lack of investment in accountability mechanisms and weak institutional commitment to implementation.

In relation to the MoIA, international community and donors:

- Even though Afghan women police have expressed their preference for segregated training and gendered deployments, in general, there remains **resistance among the international community to gendered models of policing**, which has negative implications for the effective recruitment and retention of women police.[7]

---

[5] Ibid., 28.

[6] Ibid.

[7] As an example, an international adviser consulted on the matter indicated that there is some resistance to building gender-segregated training institutions, despite Afghan women expressing preference for such facilities, so that their work practice is consistent with their faith.

- There remains an **underappreciation of the importance of community-oriented and partnership policing**[8] as a key driver to creating an institution where women can be meaningfully engaged and retained.[9] Consequently, initiatives aimed at recruiting women into current policing structures and operations are likely to encounter difficulties in retaining this personnel.

The scope of the assignment did not allow for detailed attention to the security situation province-by-province, though this was included among the recommendations for future work. This is also explored in greater depth in a forthcoming publication.

Key principles arising out of a more nuanced analysis include the importance of choice and flexibility in women's (and men's) roles which is atypical of the rigid, bureaucratic nature of police organisations. Greater choice and flexibility for women is crucial for their long-term retention, especially in dynamic conflict areas and where risks to their safety is high.

Of course, part of the need for deploying women police is to provide access to justice for women in the community. But the example of Afghanistan shows that women police often choose not to work in such risky environments, resulting in many preferring to work in urban Kabul and/or in an office environment, rather than in the provinces. Consequently, local women are not afforded a route to formal justice processes and presents a moral dilemma for implementing strategies

---

[8] Partnership policing recognizes that community safety is achieved through joint efforts from multiple stakeholders, emphasizing collaboration and working together in a coordinated approach. Partnerships may be informal or formalized through Memorandums of Understanding, written protocols or other structured forms of engagement which embed accountability mechanisms. The Community-Based Policing and Post-Conflict Reform project identified *reciprocity* as an essential element of police-community partnerships. See ICT4COP. Our Approach to COP. Accessed 14 July 2021. *www.communitypolicing.eu/ehandbook/our-approach-to-cop*.

[9] See Denney, *Policing and Gender* (Geneva: DCAF, 2019).

to deploy women police. However, if women are only given a choice to work in an insecure environment or not at all, it appears that many women will choose the latter and even depart from the organisation altogether. Pragmatically then, a more flexible strategy which enables women to continue working in an office or place where they feel safer will contribute to higher retention, and subsequently, a greater pool of women police available for deployment further outside urban areas if or when it is safer for them to do so. These women police would also benefit from longer experience in the police organisation to help build their knowledge, skills and confidence, and the organisation would benefit from not having to recruit and train new officers. Nonetheless, this was not to be the case in Afghanistan with the return of the Taliban and shows progress to advance gender equity and equality is not linear or unidirectional.

The scope of the research was limited by available resources and time. Moreover, it was undertaken during the COVID19 pandemic, as well as the security situation restricted the extent of in-person interviews and site visits that could be conducted both in Kabul and further afield. The recommendations prepared in early 2021 are included as an annex.

I hope this book provides useful information for scholars and practitioners with an interest in not only Afghanistan, but also in police reform and gendered reforms in male-dominated organisations more broadly. In particular, there are lessons to learn about the importance of having in-depth knowledge of the specific cultures, religions, geographies and impacts of conflict on police reform, rather than relying on importing policies and practices from contexts which have little in common with the state in question.

Melissa Jardine, PhD.

Acknowledgements

The author is extremely grateful to the people who generously gave their time to participate in interviews, consultations and contribute to reviewing and providing feedback on the written output of the research.

I appreciate the support of UN Women Afghanistan in conducting the research and for allowing me to publish it so that there may be some benefit from sharing the findings, even though this may not be relevant to Afghanistan at this time.

Any errors in the document are mine and not a reflection of UN Women or the reviewers.

Thanks also to the following reviewers who provided feedback in early 2021: Professor Mangai Natarajan (John Jay College of Criminal Justice, The City University of New York), Associate Professor Ingrid Nyborg (Norweigian University of Life Sciences), Jane Townsley (Executive Director, IAWP), Ellie Bird Lenawurrungu (Strategic Planning Chair, IAWP), Grant Edwards (Commander (Retd. Australian Federal Police), and Oana Neagu, Senior Gender Advisor, EU Technical Assistance for Improved Policing in Afghanistan (TAIPA)/Deutsche Gesellschaft für Internationale Zusammenarbeit (GIZ) GmbH.

Acronyms and abbreviations

AAN	Afghan Analysts Network
ABP	Afghan Border Police
ALP	Afghan Local Police
AIHRC	Afghan Independent Human Rights Commission
ANDSF	Afghan National Defence and Security Forces
ANP	Afghan National Police
CEDAW	Convention on the Elimination of Discrimination Against Women
CSO	Civil Society Organizations
CSTC-A	Combined Security Transition Command-Afghanistan
DDR	Demilitarisation, disarmament and reintegration
EUPOL	European Union Police Mission in Afghanistan
FLFP	Female labour force participation
FRU	Family Response Unit
GIZ	Deutsche Gesellschaft für Internationale Zusammenarbeit/German Corporation for International Cooperation
GPPT	German Police Project Team
GIRoA	Government of the Islamic Republic of Afghanistan
IAWP	International Association of Women Police
IPCB	International Police Coordination Board

ISAF	International Security Assistance Force
MoIA	Ministry of Interior Affairs
MoWA	Ministry of Women's Affairs
NAP	1325 National Action Plan 1325
NATO	North Atlantic Treaty Organisation
NATO	RS NATO Resolution Support
NTM-A	NATO Training Mission Afghanistan
PatG	Partners across the Globe
PeM	Police-e Mardume (community police)
PTSD	Post-traumatic stress disorder
RAM	Rapid assessment methodology
SIGAR	Special Investigator General for Afghanistan Reconstruction
SSR	Security sector reform
TAIPA	Technical Advice for Improving Policing in Afghanistan
Tashkeel	MoIA staffing structure listing the number of officers designated in the ANP
UNAMA	United Nations Assistance Mission in Afghanistan
UNDP-LOTFA	United Nations Development Programme Law and Order Trust Fund for Afghanistan
UNFPA	United Nations Population Fund
UNODC	United Nations Office on Drugs and Crime
UN	Women United Nations Entity for Gender Equality and the Empowerment of Women
UNSCR	United Nations Security Council Resolution
WPS	Women, Peace and Security

Introduction

Afghanistan is one of the least developed countries in the world and a site of protracted conflict and insecurity. With an estimated 55 per cent of the population living in poverty[10] and where gross income from its opiate economy in 2019 exceeded the value of licit exports,[11] the country has a specific security environment in which to provide policing services to the public.

The United States invasion of Afghanistan to defeat the Taliban in 2001 was followed by commitments from the international community to advance gender equality—this commitment extended to women's roles in the Afghan National Defence and Security Forces (ANDSF).[12] In the twenty years of international state-building efforts since the fall of the Taliban, women's employment in Afghanistan's security sector has seen limited progress despite significant financial investment in technical support and training efforts to fulfil international obligations. In 2021, women still comprised a mere 2.6 per cent

---

10 Central Statistics Organisation, *Afghanistan Living Conditions Survey 2016–17* (Kabul: GIRoA, CSO, 2018).

11 UNODC and GIRoA, *Afghanistan Opium Survey 2019 – Socio-Economic Survey Report: Drivers, Causes and Consequences of Opium Poppy Cultivation* (February 2021), 5.

12 SIGAR, *Support for Gender Equality: Lessons from the U.S. Experience in Afghanistan* (February 2021).

or approximately 4,075 women of a total 157,000[13] workforce of the Afghan National Police (ANP).[14]

Photo: Aurora V. Alambra / UNAMA

Image 1. The Police-e-Mardume in the ANP in Bamyan province visiting schools in 2013 in Yakawlang district to implement a safety outreach campaign aimed at helping increase public trust and confidence in their work.

Although the numbers of women police in Afghanistan are small, interaction across the environments further hinders their inclusion in the ANP. Globally, policing remains a male-dominated occupation and gender inequality is a persistent universal problem. With respect to Afghanistan, the specific conditions include: an environment constituted by armed conflict, organised crime, terrorism, a government and governance practices lacking transparency and accountability, endemic corruption, and societal values and localised cultural norms which can devalue and restrict women's rights; all of these conditions coalesce to constrain women's participation in the security sector.

---

[13] 157,000 is used here, however, it is likely to be significantly lower due to attrition and recent reports place it at about 130,000 in 2021

[14] Gender and Human Rights (2021).

In the Afghan context, which includes the impending withdrawal of international troops and potentially less ability to exert pressure or provide support towards advancing women's rights, how can gender-responsive security sector reform be strengthened to buttress gains made to date and expand women's meaningful participation in institutions responsible for public safety and security?

This research was commissioned by UN Women Afghanistan to investigate the status of gender-responsive police reform and explore approaches to improving women's meaningful participation in the ANP. Specifically, it aims to:

- Report on the current status and representation of women in the ANP;
- Reflect on past international initiatives regarding women in policing and assess lessons learned regarding their effectiveness;
- Identify strategies for police reform that will enhance the role of women in policing, security and community safety;
- Identify strategies for communicating the importance and positive impact of women police at national, provincial and district levels; and
- Identify ways to improve the physical and psychological safety of women police at work.

The research was undertaken between December 2020 and May 2021. On April 13, 2021, President Biden announced that US troops would withdraw from Afghanistan on September 11, 2021. Subsequently, other governments released plans for withdrawing military, police and other advising and training missions by the time US forces leave, and in some cases much sooner. The departure of foreign forces means increased uncertainty of what life will be like for Afghan people, especially for women and children given that women police, judges, journalists and human rights defenders were among targeted killings in the first quarter of 2021.

Crucially, the purpose of the research is to be future-focused and to advance gender-responsive security sector reform. The research aims to provide guidance for the implementation of the Women in Police Roadmap 2021–2024 recently endorsed by the Ministry of Interior Affairs (MoIA) and other research which outlines key strategies and recommendations for gender-responsive reform[15] where recruiting and retaining women in the security sector will require immediate systematic approaches and long-term strategies.

The next section introduces the methodology for the research, followed by an overview of the current status of women in the ANP and selected key reflections on the early reform process. This is followed by examining specific career phases and issues such as recruitment, training, deployment, retention, leadership and women-oriented working conditions as well as protection and complaint mechanisms. The final section takes a broader look at selected institutional changes important for creating conditions that will facilitate gendered reforms, such as communications, people-centred institution building and officer welfare. Brief recommendations focusing on structural changes and interventions follow these sections.

Box 1.

Benefits of gender-responsive police reform in Afghanistan

The nature of policing in Afghanistan must meet the safety and security needs of all Afghan people. With deeply embedded social, cultural and traditional norms which define the role(s) of men and women, the manner in which people access justice and other policing services are heavily gendered. Though there are various forms of justice in Afghanistan, international standards for fairness,

---

[15] See, e.g., WPSO and OXFAM, *Afghan Women Police*.

equity and accessibility require greater engagement and reliance on formal justice mechanisms, such as courts. Police are an important component of the justice continuum and need victim-survivors and witnesses to engage. Women are more likely to engage if there are women working within the justice continuum. It is essential that women meaningfully participate in policing to (a) strengthen internal functioning and capability, (b) contribute to achieving the ANP mandate through improving operational effectiveness, (c) advance women's empowerment, and (d) facilitate women's access to gender-sensitive support and protection.

a. Strengthening the ANP's internal functioning and capability

There are ongoing efforts within the MoIA in regard to civilianisation and police reform to build a more effective, efficient and responsive police service.[16] To achieve this, strategic planning, public administration and management require further strengthening to ensure the institution can operate effectively from headquarters to provinces, districts and local communities.[17] Both men and women can contribute to strategic decision-making, policy development, legal advisory, training and education, administration, forensics, logistics, health and wellbeing support for officers and other skills-focused and analytical roles. Including women means that the ANP and MoIA can draw on a wider range of skills, experiences and perspectives. Improved internal functioning will help the ANP meet obligations regarding international commitments (e.g., UNSCR 1325), national laws and regulatory frameworks. It is also critical that women are integral in implementing, monitoring and the evaluation of gender-responsive security sector related reforms.

---

[16] UNDP-LOTFA, project document (unpublished, 2015).
[17] Ibid.

b. Achieving the ANP mandate and improving operational effectiveness

The ANP mandate includes: maintaining public order and security; enforcing the law; protecting individual rights and freedoms; helping and assisting victims; attracting public cooperation and preventing crimes; detecting crimes and investigating criminals.[18] Women and girls can be victims, survivors, witnesses, suspects or perpetrators of crimes. Diversifying officer composition to include more women police is essential for the ANP to achieve its mandate. This is especially significant given cultural and religious practices necessitate having officers who can access women to collect evidence and intelligence or for interrogation to solve crimes. Greater inclusion of women will improve the operational effectiveness and capabilities of the organisation.

c. Advancing women's empowerment

Women are currently excluded from participating in many of the decisions that affect their health, wellbeing, safety and security. Their employment in policing provides access to positions and processes to influence these areas. Currently, women's participation in formal employment in Afghanistan is approximately 19 per cent.[19] Given the challenges for women to work outside the home in general, their entrée into male dominated occupations, such as the police, requires targeted strategies tailored for the Afghan context to facilitate women's inclusion and increase women's access to economic opportunities.

---

[18] Ministry of Justice, "Police Law", *Official Gazette* No. 862, Kabul, September 22, 2005, art. 5.
[19] World Bank, "Labor Force Participation Rate, Female (% of Female Population Ages 15+) (Modeled ILO Estimate)", accessed April 10, 2021.

d. Facilitating women's access to gender-sensitive support and protection

Women in the community are desperately in need of gender-sensitive support and protection. Specifically, women experience multiple crises of insecurity, gender-based violence and the impacts of a COVID-19 risk environment. The United Nations Population Fund estimates 87 per cent of women in Afghanistan have been victims of at least one form of physical, sexual or psychological violence, and 62 per cent have experienced multiple forms of abuse.[20] These tragic statistics may help explain why women account for an estimated 80 per cent of attempted suicides.[21] Consequently, women have an essential role in building confidence between the police and women in providing trauma-informed policing responses in the investigation of crimes current and future against women. They are also vital in facilitating referrals to gender-sensitive health and social services and other civil society organisations (CSOs).

---

[20] United Nations Population Fund, "Prosecuting Gender-based Violence in Afghanistan", February 17, 2016, *www.unfpa.org/news/prosecuting-gender-based-violence-afghanistan*.

[21] Safi, "Why Female Suicide in Afghanistan Is So Prevalent", BBC, July 1, 2018, *www.bbc.com/news/world-asia-44370711*.

Methodology

The research adopted a qualitative method to investigate the status of gender-sensitive police reform and explore approaches to improving women's meaningful participation in the Afghan National Police. A Rapid Assessment Methodology (RAM) was adopted due to time and logistical constraints during the COVID-19 pandemic and limitations on travel to and within Afghanistan due to the security situation.[22]

To inform the analysis and research design, a desk review was undertaken including relevant research, laws and policies, published reports, as well as unpublished reports provided to the researcher.

Research and literature pertaining to the following areas were considered: post-conflict policing, human security, organisational culture, police culture, women in policing in traditional and Islamic societies, women's studies (forms of agency and resistance), community and women-oriented policing, gendered and gender-responsive policing, public health policing, partnerships/relationships policing, human rights and officer wellbeing.

---

[22] MacIntyre, "Rapid Assessment and Sample Surveys: Trade-offs in Precision and Cost", *Health Policy and Planning* 14, (1999); Natarajan, "Rapid Assessment of 'Eve Teasing' (Sexual Harassment) of Young Women During the Commute to College In India", *Crime Science* 5, 6 (2016), *https://doi.org/10.1186/s40163-016-0054-9*.

A convenience sampling method was used to identify participants. Individual interviews and consultations were held online using video conferencing technology or audio calls, as well as face-to-face interviews during a field visit to Kabul in March 2021. In some cases, questions were translated to Dari by UN Women staff and sent in writing to participants. Responses were translated to English and provided to the researcher for analysis.

Interviews and consultations were conducted with people who met the following criteria:

- Have insights into the structures and cultures of the security sector in Afghanistan.
- Have knowledge of past and current initiatives regarding women in policing in Afghanistan, their impact and lessons learned, e.g., the European Union Police Mission in Afghanistan (EUPOL), German Police Project Team (GPPT), Resolute Support (RS), United Nations Development Program (UNDP) Law and Order Trust Fund for Afghanistan (LOTFA), Deutsche Gesellschaft für Internationale Zusammenarbeit/German Corporation for International Cooperation (GIZ), Technical Advice for Improving Policing in Afghanistan (TAIPA), and embassy staff in Kabul.
- Have international expertise in security sector reform.

Table 1.   Participant sample

Participant Category	Number
International policing and/or gender experts and advisors (e.g., academics, police personnel, practitioners, analysts)	35
Afghan people working for international agencies	8
Afghan government employees (MoIA, ANP, MoWA, parliamentarians)	9
Civil society representatives	2

Participant Category	Number
Religious leaders	2
Total (women=31, men=25)	**56**

Themes addressed in interviews included:

- The structural and risk environment for policing (e.g., insecurity, insurgency and civilianisation);
- Communications;
- Officer wellbeing;
- Police–community relations;
- Organisational hierarchy and structure;
- Policies, processes and practices relating to the recruitment, selection, training, deployment, retention and promotion of women police;
- Working conditions for police and specific women-oriented approaches;
- Mechanisms for preventing, reporting and responding to harassment and discrimination; and
- Infrastructure, facilities and equipment.

Analysis and theory of change

The analysis focused on aspects of policing and security sector reform that would generate a better understanding of the structural environment that is conducive or a barrier to women's inclusion. In general, these relate to processes of civilianisation and community-oriented policing because these are the conditions under which women are more likely to participate in police work (see Annex 1). Drawing on decades of research on women's inclusion in policing, the theory of change to advance women's meaningful participation in policing was, in this research and its recommendations, underpinned by a gender equity-equality model.[23] Gendered policing models should not be viewed as inferior approaches to women's inclusion but, rather, as providing context-specific and nuanced ways to increase women's access to employment in traditionally male-dominated occupations where both women and men are socialised to new or unfamiliar ways of working. Natarajan referred to gendered policing as a 'backdoor to equality' and is a culturally and gender-responsive framework for advancing women's rights in some societies in the short-term[24] while aiming to fulfil United Nations goals for gender equality over the long-term.[25]

The research was approved by the MoIA through UN Women Afghanistan. Limitations of the research include that it is a brief review conducted over a short time frame. Given Afghanistan's complex ethnic and cultural composition, a more in-depth analysis would cover provincial and district differences in more nuanced ways. Furthermore, limited interviews with serving policewomen (and men) were conducted. For this research to gather more recent and focused insights more interviews would be highly advantageous. The report does, however, draw on numerous publications from other sources[26] and these have enabled greater understanding and insight.

---

[23] See Natarajan, *Women Police*, 163; Strobl, "Towards a 'Women-Oriented' Approach".

[24] Natarajan, *Women Police*.

[25] Strobl, "Towards a 'Women-Oriented' Approach".

[26] AIHRC, *Situation of Women Employed in Defense and Security Sectors* (Autumn 2017); APPRO, *Women in Afghan National Police: A Baseline Assessment* (2014); JICA and GIWPS, *Case study on Afghanistan: Strengthening the Afghan National Police: Recruitment & Retention of Women Officers* (2016); Murray, *Report on the Status of Women in the Afghan National Police*, 2005; Oxfam, "Women and the Afghan Police" (briefing paper, 2013); UNDP, *Policewomen Census*; WPSO and Oxfam, *Afghan Women Police*.

Background regarding women police in traditional and Islamic societies

Police institutions do not exist in a vacuum; they are embedded within societies and reflect wider societal norms. Even where significant legal and institutional mechanisms are implemented to support gender equality in policing, they interact in a dialogic with the community and societal expectations of gender roles which can underpin the stability of gendered power relations and constrain the pace and nature of change.

Since the 1990s, research on enhancing women's participation in policing[27] and the military[28] has shown that strategies and approaches need to take local variables into account, especially given the significant role social and cultural norms play in shaping the nature of women's economic participation in the formal sector in general.

In traditional and Islamic societies, pathways to or aspirations regarding gender equality can vary with conceptions of 'equal but

---

[27] Natarajan, "Women Police Units in India: A New Direction", *Police Studies* 19, 2 (1996).
[28] Segal, "Women's Military Roles Cross-Nationally: Past, Present, and Future", *Gender and Society* 9, 6 (1995); Iskra et al., "Women's Participation in Armed Forces Cross-Nationally: Expanding Segal's Model", *Current Sociology* 50, 5 (2002).

different' being foregrounded by women in paramilitary organisations.[29] While women should have equal access to the full range of policing functions if they choose to pursue them, some women prefer gender-specific arrangements because they find purpose in this work or until they grow in confidence, particularly in more traditional societies.[30]

While women police and women who aspire to be police around the globe face many shared challenges,[31] variations in local contexts confront different opportunities and constraints. Natarajan reported that women police in the state of Tamil Nadu in India expressed general satisfaction working in all-women's units and that women enjoyed responding to the needs of other women, being able to balance work with family duties and were free of sexual harassment from male colleagues.[32] Natarajan asserts that gender-sensitive responses to gender-based violence (i.e., segregated or specialist units) also contribute to more women pursuing policing as a career and, in turn, increases the police's capability in addressing gender-based violence.[33] This does not mean full integration is not an aim but, rather, that progress towards

---

[29] INTERPOL, UN Women and UNODC, *Women in Law Enforcement in the ASEAN Region* (2020); Murray, review of *Women Policing Across the Globe: Shared Challenges and Successes in the Integration of Women Police Worldwide*, by C. Rabe-Hemp and V. Garcia, *Police Practice and Research* 21, 5 (2020), https://doi.org/10.1080/15614263.2020.176 5118; Natarajan, *Women Police*.

[30] Chu and Abdalla, "Self-efficacy Beliefs and Preferred Gender Role in Policing: An Examination of Policewomen's Perceptions in Dubai, the United Arab Emirates", *British Journal of Criminology* 54, 3 (2014); Natarajan, "Women Police"; Strobl, "The Women's Police Directorate in Bahrain: An Ethnographic Exploration of Gender Segregation and the Likelihood of Future Integration", *International Criminal Justice Review* 18, 1 (2008) and "Progressive or Neo-Traditional? Policewomen in Gulf Cooperation Council (GCC) Countries", *Feminist Formations* 22, 3 (2010).

[31] Rabe-Hemp and Garcia, eds., *Women Policing across the Globe: Shared Challenges and Successes in the Integration of Women Police Worldwide* (Rowman & Littlefield, 2020).

[32] Natarajan, "Women Police Units".

[33] Natarajan and Babu, "Women Police Stations: Have They Fulfilled Their Promise?" *Police Practice and Research* 21, 5 (2020), doi:10.1080/15614263.2020.1809827.

it may be slow and nuanced in order to truly reflect the needs of the population.

Ensuring women have access to gendered roles in policing contributes to attracting, recruiting and retaining more women police, which is especially true in traditional and Islamic societies.[34] In reference to the Gulf Cooperation Council countries context, Strobl theorises that, whereas integrated approaches are susceptible to reversion due to political cycles, segregated or specialised units are more stable,[35] and thus more likely to be successful in retaining female officers. Indeed, there are examples where policies to integrate women to perform the same roles as men have been reversed or led to difficulty retaining women—especially when the work is regimented, militarised and inflexible—because these working conditions can be unsatisfying for women (as experienced in India,[36] Thailand[37] and the Philippines[38]). This has relevance for other jurisdictions where segregation between genders is prominent for social, cultural or religious reasons.

Scholars of gendered policing models regard these approaches as more suitable and sustainable for traditional and Islamic societies

---

[34] Garcia, *Women in Policing Around the World: Doing Gender and Policing in a Gendered Organization* (New York: Routledge, 2021); Pervin, "Women in Leadership in the Police Administration of Bangladesh: A Review" (conference Paper, 6th International Law Enforcement and Public Health Conference, 2021).

[35] Strobl, "Progressive or Neo-Traditional?", 70.

[36] Natarajan, *Women Police.*

[37] For a recent example, the Royal Thai Police Cadet Academy first enrolled women in 2009 following changes to the Criminal Procedure Code 2008 which was amended to include requirements for same-sex body searches and the need for women police to respond to female and child victims of crime. The working conditions were inflexible leading to difficulties with retention (Fullerton, "Thai Police Academy Bans Women from Enrolling", *The Guardian*, September 5, 2018, www.theguardian.com/world/2018/sep/05/thai-police-academy-bans-women-from-enrolling). In 2018, a government instruction amended selection criteria which could not be met by women, thus, they could no longer enrol. See INTERPOL, UN Women and UNODC, *Women in Law Enforcement.*

[38] See, e.g., INTERPOL, UN Women and UNODC, *Women in Law Enforcement.*

rather than standalone integrated ones (see Annex 1).[39] The specific combination of gendered and integrated approaches for any context necessarily depends on the environment and the interaction of power dynamics in a particular place.

---

[39] Murray, review of *Women Policing*; Natarajan, *Women Police*; Strobl, "Towards a 'Women-Oriented' Approach".

International and national legal frameworks relating to policing and gender

The Government of Islamic Republic of Afghanistan (GIRₒA) has committed to implementing United Nations Security Council resolutions relating to women, peace and security (e.g., UNSCR 1325) and other international frameworks that require women's meaningful participation in security sector reform.

Box 2.

UNSCR 2151 (2014) on the need for national ownership of security sector reform

1. Underscores the importance of women's equal and effective participation and full involvement in all stages of the security sector reform process, given their vital role in the prevention and resolution of conflict and peacebuilding, and in strengthening civilian protection measures in security services, including the provision of adequate training for security personnel, the inclusion of more women in the security sector, and effective vetting processes in order to exclude perpetrators of sexual violence from the security sector.

Other international and national frameworks include:

- Convention on the Elimination of Discrimination Against Women (CEDAW), signed in 1980 and ratified in 2003 without reservations;
- Afghan Constitution 2004;
- National Action Plan on Women, Peace and Security 2015–2022;
- MoIA Strategic Plan 2015–2019;
- Afghan National Police Strategy 2010;
- Afghan Police Law 2005;
- MoIA Gender Policy 2018;
- MoIA Empowering the Women in Police: From Words to Action Roadmap 2021–2024;
- Law on Eliminating Violence Against Women (EVAW) 2009.

The "Ten-Year Vision for the Afghan National Police" (2013–2023) aimed to win "public confidence by the use of community policing approaches to deliver policing services to the people of Afghanistan";[40] however, a lack of investment and the extent of ongoing insecurity and uncertainty in Afghanistan creates a challenging environment to achieve these, and subsequently, gendered reforms.

In 2021, the MoIA published "Empowering the Women in Police: From Words to Action Roadmap 2021-2024" (hereinafter the Women in Police Roadmap 2021–2024). The Roadmap was developed by representatives from the Gender, Human Rights and Children's Directorate of the MoIA, the Gender and Human Rights Technical Working Group (composed of advisors from local and international agencies) and findings from the Policewomen Conference and consultation held in the MoIA compound in February 2020.

---

[40] Ministry of Interior Affairs, "Ten-Year Vision for the Afghan National Police" (2013–2023), *https://moi.gov.af/en/vision-mission-0*.

The Roadmap outlines six strategic priorities and three goals (see Box 3) which span issues relating to women police as well as enhancing access to justice for women and service seekers, reducing human rights violations against women and strengthening delivery of services for women, among others. The Roadmap includes a course of action, priorities and focus outline for 2021–2024 and an accompanying implementation plan. The Roadmap states that the annual action plan will be monitored and evaluated by the General Directorate of Monitoring and Evaluation of the MoIA.

Box 3.

Empowering the Women in Police:
From Words to Action Roadmap 2021-2024

Strategic priorities

1. Improve the representation of women in the police
2. Develop the capacities and competencies of women police
3. Enhance the roles, positioning and visibility of women police
4. Cultivate a gender sensitive work environment
5. Assimilate gender learning into police training
6. Improve public perceptions of policewomen.

SMART goals

1. Ensure justice and gender equality for all male and female staff of the Ministry of Interior Affairs in order to form a safe and effective work environment.
2. Increase the number of professional and capable women within the leadership and executive body of the ministry by 10% until 2024.
3. Increase the number of women in the Afghanistan National Police force to 5% by 2024.

Women in the Afghan National Police

Brief overview of reform, statistics and demographics

In Afghanistan, the first women police were enlisted in 1967 and worked, albeit in small numbers, up until the Taliban rule in the 1990s. Women were again recruited after the fall of the Taliban in 2001 and by 2005 there were 164 women police. Women were enrolled in greater numbers in policing after the international community turned its gaze to the issue after 2008.[41]

In April 2002, the donor community for Afghanistan held a meeting in Geneva to determine responsibilities and mandates for security sector reform. Five pillars for reform were identified and donor countries were assigned as follows: training (Germany); counter-nar-cotics (United Kingdom); prosecutions and the justice system (Italy); building the Afghan National Army (ANA) (United States); and demilitarisation, disarmament and reintegration (DDR) (Japan).

---

[41] The history and development of policing in Afghanistan has been well documented and only selected details are included in this report; see, e.g., Friesendorf, "Insurgency and Civilian Policing: Organizational Culture and German Police Assistance in Afghanistan", *Contemporary Security Policy* 34, 2 (2013); Murray, "Police-building in Afghanistan: A Case Study of Civil Security Reform", *International Peacekeeping* 14, 1 (2007); RUSI and FPRI, *Reforming the Afghan National Police* (2009). See also Suroush, *Assessing EUPOL Impact on Afghan Police Reform (2007–2016)* (Afghanistan Research and Evaluation Unit, January 2018).

The division of these pillars is important because the lack of collaboration, especially between Germany and the US, has been attributed to the lack of conceptual clarity regarding police reform and security and an asymmetrical focus on militarisation and counterinsurgency. The two main approaches of police reform to emerge were often conflicting: the German mandate joined the European Union Police Mission in Afghanistan (EUPOL) which focused on training and civilianisation, and, the NATO Training Mission-Afghanistan and Combined Security Transition Command-Afghanistan (NTM-A/CSTC-A) which focused on building militarised capacity among police to counterinsurgencies.

Implementation of the MoIA Strategic Plan 2018–2021 included some structural reorganisation of the ANP by transferring the semi-military capacities to the Ministry of Defense, although the ANP still has some way to go to transform to a civilian policing service. This situation is further problematised by the impending withdrawal of US and NATO Resolution Support (RS) coalition forces.

Due to the limited capacity of the MoIA, the United Nations Development Programme's Law and Order Trust Fund for Afghanistan (UNDP-LOTFA) provides significant support for reform efforts, including paying police salaries. LOTFA's project includes institutional and officer development components with emphasis on rule of law, human rights and gender-responsive and community-based policing and partnerships policing principles[42] to

---

[42] Partnerships policing recognises that community safety is achieved through multiple stakeholders, emphasising collaboration and working together in a coordinated approach. Partnerships may be informal or formalised through memorandums of understanding, written protocols and other structured forms of engagement which embed accountability mechanisms. The Community-Based Policing and Post-Conflict Reform project (referred to as ICT4COP) identified *reciprocity* as an essential element of police-community partnerships. See *www.communitypolicing.eu/ehandbook/our-approach-to-cop/*.

address gaps identified and in support of strengthening democratic policing.[43]

In 2010, amid significant pressure to advance gender equality as a core component of international missions in Afghanistan, the MoIA announced that it would aim to reach 10 per cent women in the ANP by 2014; consulting empirical evidence from other traditional and Islamic societies prior to setting such a target would have revealed it as too ambitious and unrealistic.[44] Evidently, the target could not be achieved and was subsequently revised to 5 per cent women police by 2024.[45]

In 2021, women comprised approximately 2.6 per cent of the ANP or 4,075 officers. Three-quarters (73.77%) of women police are among non-commissioned officer ranks of patrol officer (40.02%) and sergeant (35.75%) (see Figure 1).

Women's presence in the ANP is relatively new with 59 per cent of officers joining between 2013 and 2017.[46] Reforms implemented by MoIA have helped to increase the number of women in the ANP over the past decade. However, while retention is reported as a significant issue,[47] attrition data is scarce.

In 2018, there were two (0.4%) and 22 (0.9%) women holding the ranks of general (out of 483) and colonel (out of 2,350), respectively.[48] In 2021, there were no women generals, one brigadier general and only seven colonels.[49] Some senior ranking women have retired although it is not clear why there are fewer women present above the rank of colonel even though overall numbers of police women have increased.

---

[43]   UNDP-LOTFA, project document.
[44]   Murray, "Police-building in Afghanistan".
[45]   Ministry of Interior Affairs, Women in Police Roadmap 2021–2024.
[46]   UNDP, *Policewomen Census*, 16.
[47]   SIGAR, *Support for Gender Equality*.
[48]   WPSO and OXFAM, *Afghan Women Police*, 8.
[49]   Gender and Human Rights (2021).

Percentage of women in the ANP by rank, 2021

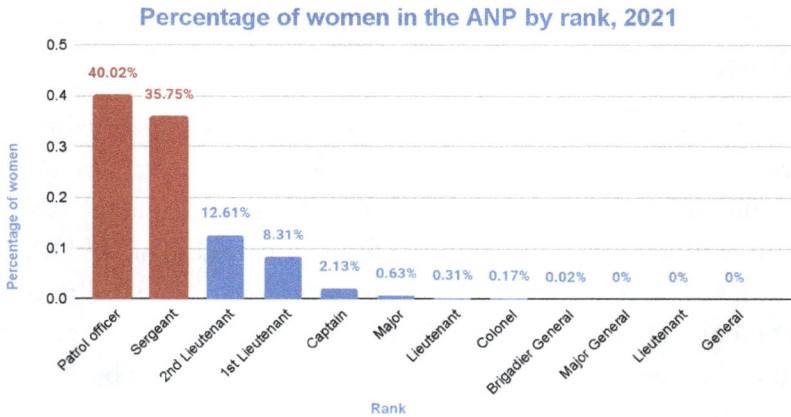

Source: Provided to the author by the Gender and Human Rights Technical Working Group, Afghanistan, March 2021.

Figure 1. Percentage of women in the ANP by rank, 2021

The dominant age category for women police is 25–34 years (see Figure 2) and 62 per cent are married (See Figure 3); 70 per cent of women police have children.[50]

Age distribution of Afghan women police, 2018

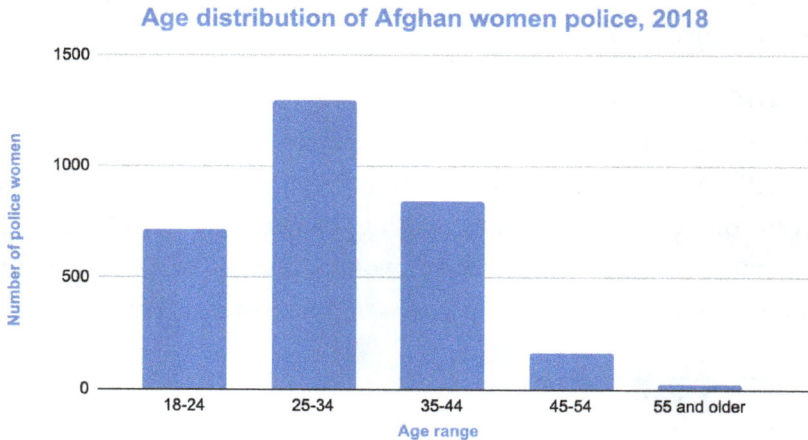

Source: UNDP, *Policewomen Census*, 12.

Figure 2. Age distribution of Afghan women police, 2018

_____

50   UNDP, *Policewomen Census*, 4.

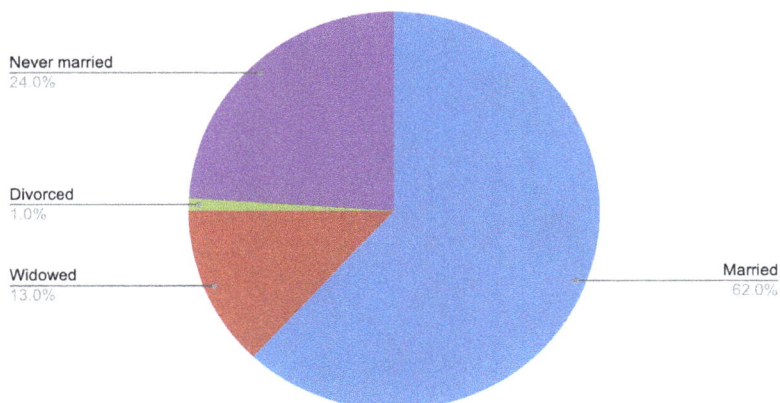

Source: UNDP, *Policewomen Census*, 13.

Figure 3.   Marital status of Afghan women police, 2018

There are numerous ethnic groups represented in Afghanistan with the largest proportion identifying as Pashtun (42%), followed by Tajik (27%), Hazara (9%), Uzbek (9%), Aimak (4%) and Turkmen (3%), among others.[51] These ethnic groups are represented differently among women police with Tajik (40%) and Hazara (31%) making up greater numbers than Pashtuns (20%) despite the latter comprising a greater proportion of population overall (see Figure 4). An explanation for this variation is that the different religious, cultural and gender norms practiced among the ethnic groups influence women's participation in formal work or activities outside the home, as well as different economic needs.

Similarly, even though Sunni Muslims account for 80–89 per cent of the population and Shia 10–19 per cent,[52] in the Afghanistan National Policewomen Census Survey 2018, 65 per cent of women identified as Sunni Muslim and 34 per cent as Shia.[53]

---

[51]   World Population Review, "Afghanistan Population 2019", accessed May 22, 2021.

[52]   Ibid.

[53]   UNDP, *Policewomen Census*, 13.

Ethnicity of Afghan Policewomen, 2018

Other
4.0%

Uzbek
5.0%

Pashtun
20.0%

Tajik
40.0%

Hazara
31.0%

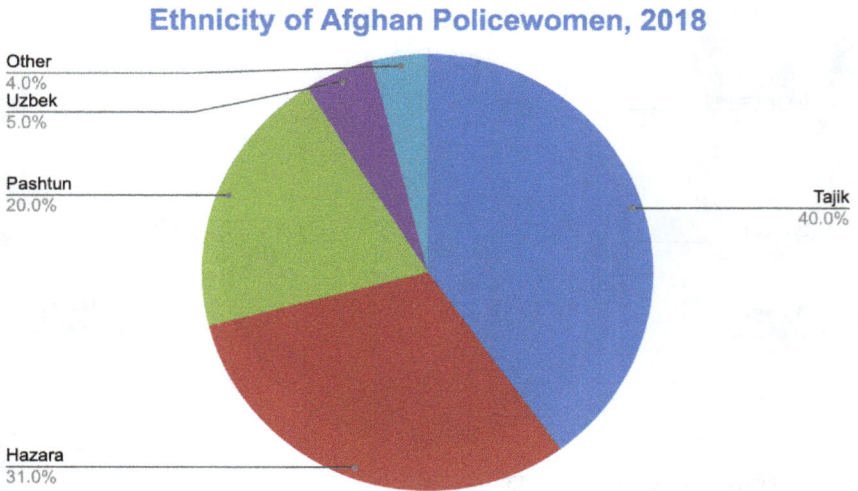

Source: UNDP, *Policewomen Census*, 14.

Figure 4.   Ethnicity of Afghan women police, 2018

Low levels of literacy in Afghanistan impact upon the pool of potential applicants for the ANP and the nature of the work they do once employed. While literacy levels among the general population are improving (43%), women's literacy remains low at 30 per cent, with men's literacy at 55 per cent in 2018.[54] Consequently, it is a competitive environment to recruit educated women, especially in Kabul, who have more access to higher paying and higher status occupations. Figure 5 shows that 27 per cent of women police have no formal education and only 5 per cent have a college degree.

---

[54]   UNESCO, "UNESCO Stands with all Afghans to Ensure Youth and Adults in Afghanistan, Especially Women and Girls, Achieve Literacy and Numeracy by 2030", press release, September 8, 2021, *https://en.unesco.org/news/unesco-stands-all-afghans-ensure-youth-and-adults-afghanistan-especially-women-and-girls*.

Education levels among Afghan women police, 2018

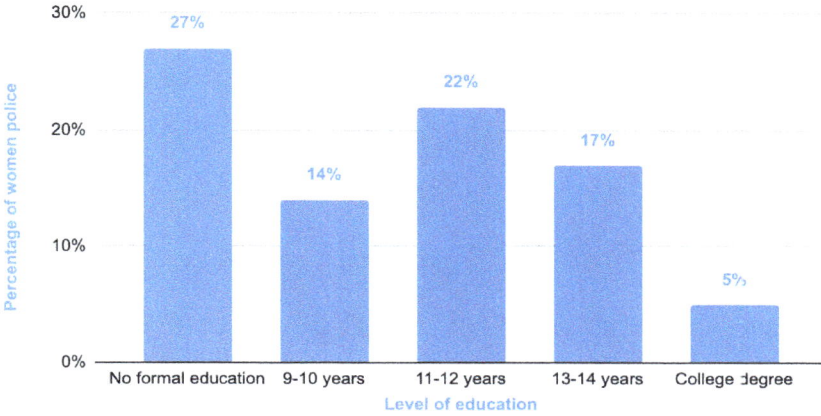

Source: UNDP, *Policewomen Census*, 13.

Figure 5.   Education levels among Afghan women police, 2018

The Afghanistan National Policewomen Census Survey 2018 indicates that 26 per cent of women are deployed as 'searchers' (i.e., conduct body pat-down searches of women at checkpoints and for border control), 9 per cent in Family Response Units (FRUs) and 8 per cent in other Criminal Investigations Departments (CIDs).[55] Women are also present in the Gender, Human Rights and Child Rights Directorate (6%), the Health Department (6%) and the Afghan National Police Academy (6%) (see Figure 6).[56]

---

[55]   Ministry of Interior Affairs, Women in Police Roadmap 2021–2024.
[56]   Ibid.

Women police officer assignment by department, 2018

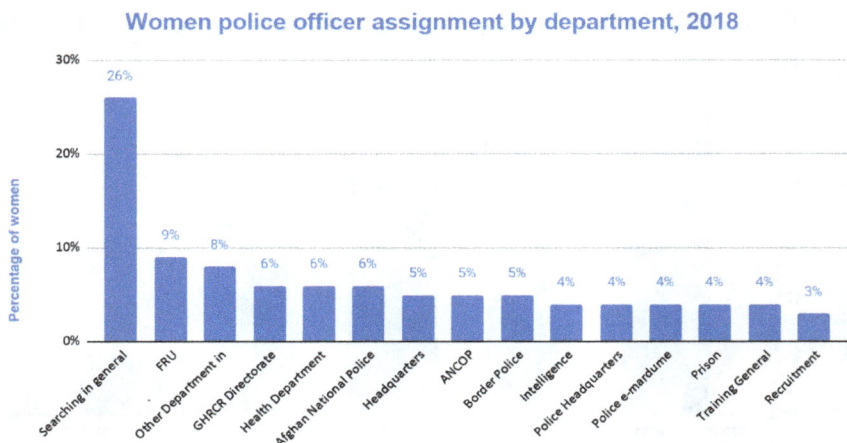

Source: UNDP, *Policewomen Census*, 17–18.

Figure 6.   Women police officer assignment by department, 2018

Almost half (48%) of all police women work in Kabul, followed by Herat (8%), Balkh (5%), Kandahar (4%) and Kunduz (6%).[57] Some women are reluctant to work in their assigned positions in provinces due to safety concerns, and instead work from a location in Kabul. Indeed, there may have been a deterioration in the coverage of women police outside Kabul due to a worsening security situation[58] and increased targeted killings. While there are financial incentives for women to work in some provinces, it appears this compensation is not enough to outweigh women's concerns in many cases. A study on the relationship between terror attacks and women's employment in Afghanistan indicates there is a correlation between the number of attacks and a decline in women's labour force participation in the aftermath.[59] This likely has implications for the deployment of women to areas with lower levels of security, especially outside Kabul, resulting in less effective policing. Nonetheless, the bombing at the entrance of

---

[57]   UNDP, *Policewomen Census*, 4, 8.

[58]   WPSO and OXFAM, *Afghan Women Police*.

[59]   Cahalan, Gitter and Fletcher, "Terrorism and Women's Employment in Afghanistan", *Oxford Development Studies* 48, 2 (2020).

Sayed Al-Shohada High School in Shiite Muslim neighbourhood in Kabul on May 8, 2021, which killed more than 85 people, mostly girls aged between 11–15, may not only affect the willingness of families to send their daughters to get an education, it may also compound concerns about risk for working women.

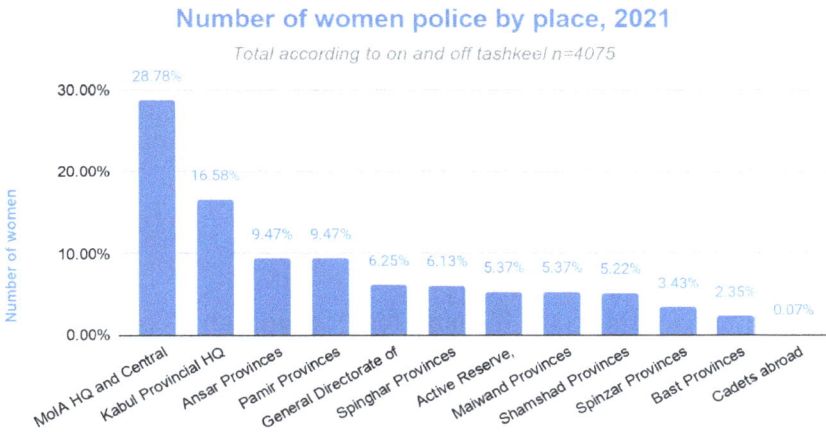

Number of women police by place, 2021

Total according to on and off tashkeel n=4075

Source: Provided to the author by the Gender and Human Rights Technical Working Group, Afghanistan, March 2021.

Figure 7.   Number of women police by place, 2021

The data in this section illustrates that women in the ANP are found in greater proportions among the non-commissioned officer ranks, and perform 'searching' functions or work in office-based roles in police stations in Kabul province or at MoIA headquarters.

Reflection on past initiatives and lessons learned

An emphasis on state security rather than civil and human security has stymied the police contribution to peacebuilding in Afghanistan and reform to reflect civilian policing. Unlike the military, which acts to protect the state, policing derives its legitimacy of power from the community, policing by consent and rule of law.[60] The early and likely ongoing militarised focus of the ANP has dual implications with regard to gendered reforms: firstly, militarised policing is generally less conducive to women's inclusion and, secondly, it detracts from the importance of building the relational aspects of police institutional capability needed to underpin efforts to recruit, retain and deploy women police in an Islamic society over the long term. Some key lessons from the early stages of policing reform and their implications for gender-sensitive reform include the following:

A knowledge gap and disconnect among and between police and gender advisors

The US Special Inspector General for Afghanistan Reconstruction (SIGAR) 2021 reported on lessons learned in their support for gender equality, highlighting that "a failure to anticipate or appreciate Afghan cultural context … undercut" efforts to support women and girls,[61] a reflection equally relevant to policing.[62] Fifteen years ago, Murray identified a knowledge gap among international deployments in Afghanistan with respect to police advisors who have tactical rather than strategic knowledge, and gender advisors who lack understanding of police institutions and cultures.[63] Murray argued this knowledge gap and disconnect between policing and gender advisors contributed to an inability to develop a coherent strategy for police reform, and that gendered reforms were undertaken in parallel to—rather than as part of—wider reform efforts such as the design of the *tashkeel*, the organising structure for the ANP[64] which informs the placement and deployment of police officers across Afghanistan.

---

[60] Murray, "Police-building in Afghanistan".
[61] SIGAR, *Support for Gender Equality*, 153–4.
[62] Murray, *Report on the Status of Women* and "Police-building in Afghanistan".
[63] Ibid.
[64] Murray, "Police-building in Afghanistan".

The lack of gender perspective in the design of the *tashkeel* was a missed opportunity to facilitate gender-inclusive reform.[65] The government of Afghanistan approved the *tashkeel* in November 2005 and adopted it as the ANP force-structure planning document the following month. The *tashkeel* designates positions in the ANP as P1 (men only), P2 (male and female) and P3 (women only). There are currently 5,000 P3 positions for women only (mostly among lower ranks).[66] However, given there are only 4,075 women officers, men currently fill some P3 roles. The Women in Police Roadmap 2021–2024 (along with other strategic documents relating to the ANDSF) aims to designate all positions as P2, for men and women, in future.[67] Until recently, officers had to find their own post-graduation placement which resulted in women facing discrimination from police chiefs who did not support women police or overlooked them in favour of men. Now, based on the recently approved policy, women are assigned to positions determined by the MoIA.

The distribution of women police across ranks (Figure 1) and functions (Figure 6) shows they perform low-status roles and dominate non-commissioned officer ranks. However, it is common in other traditional and Islamic societies for women to enter policing in greater proportions at commissioned officer rank to undertake specialised or administrative roles. By contrast, in rank structures common in Anglo-American police institutions women are deployed after graduation to operational functions, from where they work their way up through non-commissioned officer ranks, and possibly onto commissioned officers. Given the cultural and policing context of Afghanistan, applying a gender perspective to identify appropriate *tashkeel* assignments for women police is a key protection and retention measure. A

---

[65]   Ibid.

[66]   WPSO and OXFAM, *Afghan Women Police*.

[67]   In Taiwan, desegregation ironically gave men more access to roles previously dominated by women than vice versa; see Cao et al., *Policing in Taiwan: From Authoritarianism to Democracy* (Routledge, 2014): 178.

revised *tashkeel* is due to be endorsed in 2021 and includes input from gender advisors who are *tashkeel* committee members.

Donor countries can also pursue an approach that reflects their interests rather than the interests of the donor recipient, in this case, the Afghan people.[68] Current and former international police trainers and gender advisors consulted for this study corroborated this view in relation to approaches to deploy women police. One participant of an international agency said:

> *[The international community] wanted to push to get more women in the police and to get women working alongside men like they do in Western countries. In Afghanistan, women have generally not been in the workplace anyway and I think the early approach has resulted in some backlash and potentially setback progress.*

Another participant from an international agency reflected on the "bad reputation" (i.e., insulting women by targeting their morality) that women police have in Afghanistan:

> *I think we, the international community, have a lot to answer for in relation to the bad reputation women have as police officers. When the 10 per cent target for women was set and the focus was just on numbers [of women recruited] it sent a lot of vulnerable women into a situation where they were exploited. There was no plan for their deployment.*

The EU Annual Action Programme 2018[69] for funding security sector reform in Afghanistan acknowledges the issue of causing "unintended

---

68 Friesendorf, "Insurgency and Civilian Policing".

69 EU Annual Action Programme 2018 part 2, 2019 part 1 and 2020 part 1 in favour of Afghanistan to be financed from the general budget of the Union, Ref. Ares (2018) 3231251 – 19/06/2018.

consequences" as a result of recruiting women without adequate basic qualifications as a (low) risk. This is an important acknowledgement and recent efforts are seeking to mitigate risks to women, though institutional capacity of the MoIA, MoWA and Afghanistan Independent Human Rights Commission (AIHRC) remains limited in holding to account perpetrators who harass, assault or exploit women.[70]

In the early stages of building infrastructure, such as police training institutions, little attention was paid to facilities needed for women, especially the need for gender segregated facilities.[71] Significant investment has since been made to accommodate women's needs in relation to bathrooms, changing rooms and rest areas; however, women police have continued to express the importance of gender segregated training facilities. Yet, in 2021, resistance to segregated training institutions in the international community persists, driven by arguments that, since men and women will have to work together in future, there is no need for investing in (more) training facilities.[72] This highlights the importance of in-depth planning and consultative processes at the outset because it would have identified the strategic and long-term value of gender-segregated police training in an Islamic society, especially given that women require permission from family to join the police and enter this professional space.[73] Even though having men and women working together is an important future aim, the resistance to investing in gender-sensitive training institutions lacks an appreciation of the slow pace of change in gender power relations and susceptibility to reversion even if progress is made.

---

[70] WPSO and OXFAM, *Afghan Women Police.*
[71] AIHRC, *Situation of Women.*
[72] Personal communication with international advisor, March 2021.
[73] Denney, *Policing and Gender.*

Box 4.

International advisors in post-conflict countries and gender-responsive police reform

There is a risk that when international advisors seek to enhance the role of women in policing or to mainstream gender in organisations, in post conflict countries, they draw upon their 'here and now' as the baseline for defining the shape and nature of women's roles. They often fail to reflect on the journey undertaken, the lessons learned and the compromises to get here.

Well intended demands and hyped expectations of women fulfilling the same roles as men, equipped with lethal weapons, tasked to patrol major supply routes still under threat of attack and work in confined spaces in close proximity of men create the perfect storm for failure.

In such environments, meaningful roles for women look different. Their presence, in uniform, carrying out basic functions within the policing space is a milestone for the future. Over months and years, their presence becomes the new norm, an acceptable presence in a male dominated space, moving freely without challenge or exploitation.

As advisors, we must commit to understanding the complexity of the problem and not simply transition what success looks like for us into a solution. Establishing women into some roles might take a generation, but their presence within the police station, identified within communities, is the foundation for that success.

Ellie Bird Lenawarungu, Strategic Planning Chair, International Association of Women Police[74]

---

[74] Personal communication within the framework of the research in May 2021.

Due to a confluence of factors, the approach to including women in the ANP appears to have initially followed Brown's universalist model[75] rather than a model suited to the local context and stated preferences and aspirations of Afghan women and has likely contributed to high levels of attrition. Societies with more traditional views of gender norms are ill-suited to a universalist model of integration,[76] especially in the early stages of women's inclusion. Annex 1 includes Natarajan's comparison of integrated and gendered policing models in relation to policing styles and the status and self-image of women officers which has relevance to the Afghan context. Indeed, in discussions with the MoIA for this research, several participants expressed a desire to learn more about strategies to recruit and deploy women police from other Islamic countries rather than Western countries. This is also in line with operative paragraph 18 of UNSCR 2151 (2014) which emphasises the importance of South-South exchange and cooperation in relation to security sector reform.

Critically though, women in government and community leadership roles and women police should be involved in decision-making about their prospective roles. Even though policing in Afghanistan does entail significant risks, there are risks for both men and women. Risks for women should not be used to stall their inclusion into the security sector,[77] but the nature of their inclusion should be context specific and informed by the needs and realities of the women affected. Indeed, women have an important transformational role in

---

[75] Brown, "European Policewomen: A Comparative Research Perspective", *International Journal of Sociology of Law* 25 (1997).

[76] Garcia, *Women in Policing*; Kim and Gerber, "Attitudes Toward Gender Integration in Policing: A Study of Police Cadets in China", *International Journal of Law Crime and Justice* 57 (2019); Strobl, "Progressive or Neo-Traditional?" and "Towards a 'Women-Oriented' Approach".

[77] Gordon, McHugh and Townsley, "Risk Versus Transformational Opportunities in Gender-Responsive Security Sector Reform", *Journal of Global Security Studies* (June 2020), *https://doi.org/10.1093/jogss/ogaa028*.

the security sector to ensure that women, men, girls and boys are all supported and protected.

During consultations for this research, it appears that the knowledge gaps between policing and gender advisors identified by Murray have significantly reduced and current initiatives are cognisant of the cultural and social context in Afghanistan that underpins gender-sensitive reforms. However, gendered reforms and initiatives in general continue to be considered as they relate to human resources practices such as recruitment criteria, training provision, individually focused incentives and professional development opportunities. There remains an underappreciation of the relationship between community-oriented and partnership policing as a key driver to creating an institution where women can be meaningfully engaged and retained.[78] In Afghanistan, this requires greater collaboration between the MoIA's directorates and departments leading and playing a role in implementing the Women in Police Roadmap, in addition to, for example, the technical working groups on gender and human rights and those relating to institutional reform and citizen services.

Challenges associated with deploying international police and gender advisors include short-term deployments which afford little time to build mentoring relationships with Afghan police leaders and counterparts who are also reshuffled periodically. Murray also noted that international advisors may not necessarily be people with a superior skill set, but are people who are available to be absent from their usual role and other commitments.[79]

---

[78] See Denney, *Policing and Gender*.
[79] Murray, "Police-building in Afghanistan".

Donor conditions and a narrow view on what constitutes building police capability and implications for gender-responsive reform

Security institutions, such as the police, influence and are influenced by the environment in which they exist. People-centred institution building focuses on changing the day-to-day practices of police so that new norms evolve and fresh schemas of experience emerge (i.e., understanding of occupational values) which are necessary for transitioning from a military to community-oriented police service.[80] On-the-job experiential learning is an essential part of security sector reform,[81] although reform efforts in Afghanistan have been critiqued for a tendency to do what is measurable (e.g., training courses) rather than what is necessary (e.g., improving policing quality).[82] Another risk is the potential for the massive underinvestment in community-oriented policing, leaving the Afghan people with a quasi-military rather than police service.[83] Restrictions in Afghanistan on mobility, especially for women, make these learning opportunities a challenge; however, these methods are equally important as a structural intervention for male officers and can improve policing quality and contribute to creating an institution and occupation more attractive to women as a possible career path.

---

[80] Marks, *Transforming the Robocops: Changing Police in South Africa* (Scottsville, South Africa: University of KwaZulu-Natal Press, 2005).

[81] European Security and Defence College, *Civilian Coordinator for Training in Security Sector Reform: ESDC EAB SSR Report on Training Requirements Analysis for Civilian CSDP Missions* (2020).

[82] Murray, "Police-building in Afghanistan".

[83] Planty and Perito, *Police Transition in Afghanistan,* Special Report 322 (United States Institute of Peace, 2013).

Box 5.

> ### The need for more strategic investment in police reform
>
> The trap [in international programming] is composed of restrictive mandates, inappropriate funding structures, and an overly narrow view of the legitimate actors in police reform, all of which falsely present ministries and governments as the only potential partners for community policing interventions. This results in a systemic lack of support for a viable and promising alternative: civil society-driven police reform.[84]

Donor conditions can take a narrow view on what constitutes professionalisation (e.g., training, rules, uniforms) which limits funding to MoIA or police institutions rather than developing the skills required by police in relation to professional judgement which calls for multi-sector and civil society engagement in the processes of professionalisation.[85] As an example, in the past, donor funding was often subject to narrow spending criteria focused strictly on training and capacity building of police in a way that failed to recognise the relational aspects of learning to be an effective police officer. Coyne and Nyborg recount the UNDP-LOTFA's rejection of funding for a project to encourage networking and relationships policing between police officers responsible for domestic violence responses and health care providers to increase mutual referrals on gender-based violence on the basis that funding could not be used to train staff from the Ministry of Public Health.[86]

---

[84] Coyne and Nyborg, "Pushing on a String? An Argument for Civil Society-driven Community Policing as Alternative to Ministry-centric Approach in Conflict-affected States", *Journal of Human Security* 16, 2 (2020): 31.

[85] Ibid.

[86] Coyne and Nyborg, "Pushing on a String?".

In sum, the elements of international police assistance in Afghanistan that have been detrimental to advancing the women, peace and security (WPS) agenda include: the prioritisation of short-term security gains through proxy forces over human security; a lack of coordination among the various actors providing assistance; and the export of norms and practices that better match the conditions of donor states than the recipient state.

Recruiting, deploying and retaining women police with diverse needs and aspirations

Women's participation in policing must be considered within the specific contexts in which they work. In traditional and Islamic societies this requires consideration of strongly held beliefs and practices regarding gender roles and norms for men and women. Notwithstanding, women have made progress in policing careers in some countries, typically through gendered career pathways, especially in the early stages of women's entrée in the occupation.

The specific security environment and power dynamics for women and policing in Afghanistan include: the presence of armed conflict and terrorist activity; organised crime, corruption and the opium economy; policing and security cultures; governance structures and practices (formal and informal); local/Islamic religious cultures; and gender structures (see Figure 8). Furthermore, the structure and composition of the MoIA following the US and NATO withdrawal is uncertain with regard to a transitional/power-sharing government or the absence of a peace agreement. These dynamics need to be considered in relation to the form, nature and pace of gender-responsive police reform in Afghanistan.

Source: Developed by M. Natarajan and M. Jardine, 2021.

Figure 8. Multifaceted environment constraints for women in policing in Afghanistan

While insights from other countries can be a useful guide for the ANP, the Afghanistan context is complex with significant variation and uncertainty across the country at intersections including: ethnic background and tribalism; religious practices and differences in 'protection' and 'control' of women; financial insecurity; and physical and psychological security. Furthermore, women are not a monolithic group, and different experiences of governance and conflict relating to age, race, class and ability cut across individual needs and realities.

During consultations for this research, which took place after the announcement of a firm September 2021 withdrawal, participants were generally pessimistic about prospects for improving women's rights and security in the absence of foreign troops (and subsequently pressure and influence) whereby holding onto and stabilising current gains for women's inclusion in policing could be considered a best-case scenario.

The following sections discuss specific career stages and elements of gender-responsive security sector reform in the ANP.

Recruitment and training

There is a current target of 5 per cent women police by 2024; however, there is considerable difficulty attracting women to become police officers. Policing is considered a low status occupation in Afghanistan with low pay at approximately USD$150 per month. As a result, people who join the police may do so as a last resort. In one study, 80 per cent of women interviewed described economic necessity as their reason for joining the police.[87] Previous research has explored women's motivations for joining the ANP[88] and identified the following drivers:

- financial security for themselves or their family;
- having a desire to become a police officer since childhood, to follow in their father's or brother's footsteps and continue a family legacy in the security forces;
- to help women, to raise awareness about women's rights and to pursue justice for female victims and socially-vulnerable people;
- being driven by difficult challenges such as poverty, sexual and gender-based violence or discrimination; and
- a pathway to a post-policing career, either through building skills or saving money for education and training.

---

[87] WPSO and OXFAM, *Afghan Women Police*.
[88] JICA and GIWPS, *Case Study on Afghanistan*; APPRO, *Women in Afghan National Police*.

In a study on female labour force participation (FLFP) in Afghanistan, security was identified as a first-order issue affecting women's willingness to leave home for work and elevated men's concern about women's mobility.[89] In the absence of increased security, the authors recommended increasing FLFP through targeted support for income-generating activities to accommodate women's safety concerns while contributing to their economic empowerment. Conservatism, social norms and religious/Islamic beliefs about gender roles, being married and level of education also shape women's participation in formal employment in Afghanistan.[90]

According to the Afghanistan National Policewomen Census Survey 2018, the most frequently cited barriers to a safe working environment were security (37%) and behaviours towards women (22%).[91] Separate bathrooms and equipment were rated lower at 12 and 11 per cent, respectively.[92]

Nonetheless, support for women to work outside the home in general, and for the army/police, has risen slightly (see Figures 9 and 10). The report noted that an increase in women in employment may be more a result of financial precarity than belief in a woman's right to work.[93]

---

[89] Desai and Li, "Analyzing Female Labor Force Participation in Afghanistan: Identifying the Key Barriers that Prevent Women from Entering the Labor Force", *Women's Policy Journal* (2016).

[90] Parlaktuna and Sidiqi, "The Effect of Socio-Cultural Norms on Female Labor Force Participation in Afghanistan", *Kadın/Woman 2000, Journal for Women's Studies* 21, 2 (2020).

[91] UNDP, *Policewomen Census*, 28.

[92] Ibid.

[93] The Asia Foundation, *A Survey of the Afghan People: Afghanistan in 2019*, 223.

Support for women working outside the home, 2019

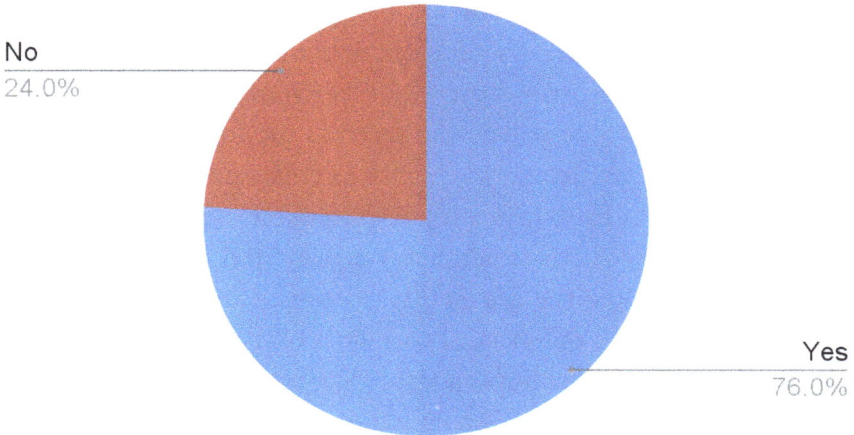

No
24.0%

Yes
76.0%

Source: Asia Foundation, *A Survey of the Afghan People*, 223.

Figure 9. Support for women working outside the home, 2019

Army/police as an acceptable place of employment for women, 2019

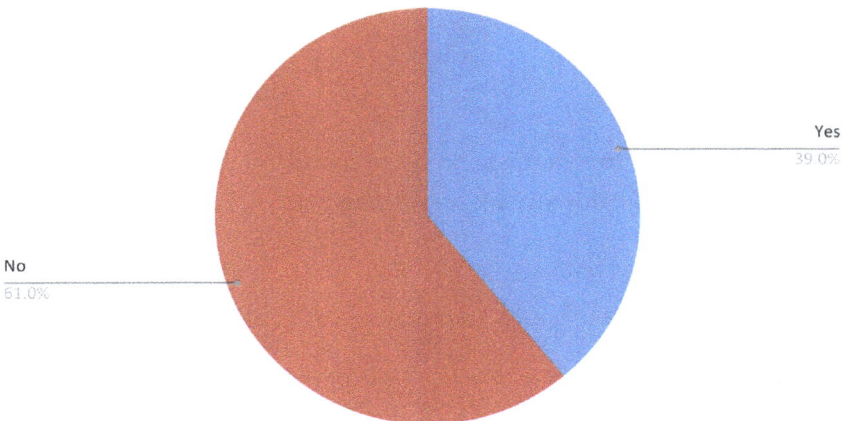

Yes
39.0%

No
61.0%

Source: Asia Foundation, *A Survey of the Afghan People*, 225.

Figure 10. Army/police as an acceptable place of employment for women, 2019

Even though the barriers to women's work in policing listed above are structural, financial incentives are offered to individuals to make policing a more attractive option for women.[94] The bonus paid to women at the point of recruitment is among the highest incentives across a range of career stages, roles, activities and provisions (see Box 6). During discussions for the research, participants reported there were few women police who received the training and education allowance to participate in English or other additional education activities. In some cases, women police were reluctant to participate in training where the instructor was a man, and there were some difficulties regarding the availability of women instructors or their willingness to travel to locations to train women. Some courses are held in the evening which was another barrier to women's participation. Moreover, some participants indicated women expressed little motivation to undertake further training. This requires more exploration, although given that women are most commonly deployed as 'searchers' and the *tashkeel* assigns few women to office-based roles (e.g., the recruitment command) they may see little benefit investing their time to gain extra skills.

Box 6.

Financial incentives to recruit, train, deploy and retain women police 2018

- Recruitment bonus
- Re-contracting bonus (extenuation of contract for a period of 3 years)
- Training and education allowance (during training)
- Instructor incentive

---

[94] Ministry of Interior Affairs, Incentives Code (MoIA, General Directorate of Police Law and Human, Child and Women's Rights Directorate, 2021).

- Retention incentive

- Childcare allowance (paid for each child until the age of 6)

- Relocation/housing allowance for deployment to provinces with few women

- Referral bonus (for serving officers to refer a woman for recruitment)

- Travel allowance for accompanying another sick female ANP officer

- Operative and night shift duty incentive (for women in special combat units of the General Command, Counter-Narcotics ministry, detention centres and night shift service in police hospitals).

Source: Ministry of Interior Affairs, Incentives Code, (MoIA, General Directorate of Police Law and Human, Child and Women's Rights Directorate, 2018).

In 2011, a trilateral agreement between Afghanistan, Turkey and Japan enabled women police cadets to undertake training at the Sivas Police Training Centre in Turkey. The UNDP-LOTFA would administer the program on Japan's behalf. Due to difficulties associated with attracting women to join the ANP, one rationale for training in Turkey was that international travel may be an incentive to prospective applicants (more on the training below). In 2020, the MoIA requested support from LOTFA to enlist an NGO to undertake a recruitment campaign for the women-only training course in Sivas.[95] Recruitment campaigns included visiting universities, women's NGOs and popular public areas to distribute leaflets and show videos to potential applicants. These campaigns aimed to recruit for specific cohorts of cadets as well as to build a database of women for future campaigns.

---

[95] Personal communication with UNDP-LOTFA staff, May 2021.

While the NGO was able to attract more candidates, the MoIA did not accept many on the list and ultimately the cost to coordinate the campaign across provinces (with limited security support from MoIA) meant not all areas could be reached and the procurement process was too long to be effective.[96]

While outsourcing the recruitment of women may seek a short-term benefit, it is not clear whether women identified through this method may have differing (i.e., realistic) expectations of their future employer, and thus impact their retention. Moreover, a structural intervention for sustainable change and long-term impact could include investing in people-centred capacity building of the MoIA recruitment command, such as a model where the NGO or LOTFA staff are co-located and have a mentoring role for MoIA officers.[97] Capacity building that includes establishing internal mechanisms for measuring the effectiveness of recruitment campaigns and system-atically assessing points of attrition in both the recruitment process and post-graduation would be beneficial.

Attracting more women in policing requires systematic immediate and long-term measures, including recruitment campaigns that are geared towards highlighting the specific contributions women can make and that align with women's motivations for pursuing employment with the police.[98] This can help overcome perceptions that women are only important in policing and the security sector to please international donors.[99]

---

[96] Ibid.

[97] UNDP-LOTFA, project document, vi.

[98] Natarajan, "Gender Equality in Law Enforcement: Make it real through Mentoring the Next Generation" (conference paper, International Association of Women Police Training Conference, Anchorage, Alaska, September 22–27, 2019).

[99] WPSO and OXFAM, *Afghan Women Police*.

Germany and the US have built training facilities for police: Germany rebuilt the Afghanistan National Police Academy (ANPA) in Kabul, and the US has built training centres in Kabul and in six regions. The Academy functions according to the Law on Military Higher Education Institutions (07/28/1394) [2015], which shapes the occupational outlook of graduates. Training centres deliver basic training and are tactically focused in, for example, firearms handling, range training, building searches, vehicle searches, drill and ceremonies, high-risk vehicle stops, defensive tactics, baton training, and handcuffing techniques.

A women-only training centre was relocated from Jalalabad to the MoIA, Kabul, and then to the Central Training Command in 2017. Still, police training institutions were largely built in a manner that is gender blind, reflecting a universal or integrated approach with an under-appreciation for the importance of women being able to practice their faith alongside a policing career. Efforts to retrofit police training institutions to accommodate women remain challenged by a preference for segregated training, thus deterring prospective women applicants.[100] Belatedly, there appears to be increased awareness among donors of the importance of gender-segregated training for women police and are common in traditional and non-western countries[101] and plans to build these facilities are being drafted.

---

[100] Personal communication with female gender advisor for an international agency, March 2021.

[101] Natarajan, *Women Police*.

Box 7.

Summary of training institutions and recruitment criteria for the ANP[102]

Afghanistan National Police Academy (4 years duration and graduate as a commissioned officer)

- 12th grade minimum education
- Aged between 18 and 35 years old
- Good physical and mental health
- Not addicted to illegal drugs
- No conviction for a term of imprisonment longer than 1 year
- Be law abiding
- No political party affiliation
- Minimum height of 1.7 m for men and 1.55 m for women
- Women must have a written consent letter from family (i.e., a male family member).

Afghanistan Police Academy (1 year and graduate as a commissioned officer)

- Bachelor degree minimum education
- Pathway to recruit and deploy officers for specialist roles e.g., economic crimes, computer sciences.

Training Centres (located in Kabul, regions and provinces; Women's Training Centres (Herat, Mazar-e-Sharif, Kinduz, Nangarhar and Kabul)

- 4–8 weeks duration
- Must have two police or local government official vouch for good character

---

[102] Must hold Afghan citizenship.

- Graduate as non-commissioned officer.

Capacity Building College (formerly Staff College)

- 1 year
- Located in Kabul
- Open to men and women (few women attend)
- Must be a serving officer
- Provides targeted training in leadership, management, human rights awareness, gender awareness, command and control, intelligence-led policing and community policing.

Other entry pathways

- Civilian appointments
- Inheriting positions through martyred police family members.

Sivas Police Training Centre, Turkey

The UNDP-LOTFA program agreement between Afghanistan, Turkey and Japan established a program to enable women police and cadets to undertake training at the Sivas Police Training Centre in Turkey. The first course commenced in 2014 and 1,152 women cadets graduated up to the end of 2019, with an expectation this will rise to 1,402 by the end of 2021. Training for cadets is typically 4–6 months, while in-service training for serving women officers is between 1–4 months. Cadet training is usually for cohorts of 250, while in-service training is for smaller groups (e.g., 25–30).

Training at Sivas is advantageous due to the safer security environment for both cadets and trainers as compared to Afghanistan which enables focus on the learning at-hand. During consultations for this research, international training was also described as an important incentive to attract and recruit more women into an unpopular organ-isation. Furthermore, the training provided by Sivas was deemed to be of superior quality to what was able to be delivered in Afghanistan. Cross-cultural and police peer-to-peer learning with a neighbouring Islamic country is also a useful strategy for enhancing the capability of the MoIA and ANP overall.

Although literacy is a prerequisite for acceptance into the training, this does not necessarily occur in practice. In theory, course graduates who have grade 12 level education are appointed as non-commissioned officers at the sergeant level, and cadets with two years or more of post-secondary education are appointed as commissioned officers at the rank of 2nd Lieutenant. In practice, there appears to be consider-able discretion as to the rank of a graduating officer.

During consultations for this research, it is clear there is considerable controversy about the Sivas training for women cadets. While the overseas training opportunity was designed as an incentive to attract more women, there is concern that it may attract women who do not intend to remain as officers following their international travel experience. Among the other concerns raised were: sexual assault and harassment of the cadets by supervising male staff; the lack of suit-ability of the training for the Afghan context; the cost of training at Sivas when it could have been invested locally; and a lack of retention of graduates, making it a poor return on investment.

Due to the challenges of recruiting women to the ANP, cadets who participate in the Sivas training are often from poor backgrounds from across Afghanistan with low levels of literacy (if literate at all), rendering them vulnerable to exploitation of various sorts. Sivas-trained cadets are on average younger (21 years old) than women who undertake training in Afghanistan (26 years old).[103] There are allegations that the substantial recruitment bonus offered as an

---

[103] UNDP, *Policewomen Census*, 18.

incentive to boost the overall numbers of women police is sometimes appropriated by senior male and female officers. Moreover, sexual assault and harassment of the cadets by superiors was described as commonplace, including cadets returning from Turkey impregnated. While specific case files were not available for the research, these concerns were held by people from the MoIA, ANP and international agencies. This raises questions about the principle of Do No Harm for cadets who enrol to become police, and women undertaking in-service training.

The suitability of Sivas training for the Afghan context is also a concern among some stakeholders. Some view the training as a good quality, standardised police training package, while others consider it lacks enough relevant information to understand and respond to the local needs in Afghanistan. The Women & Peace Studies Organisation and OXFAM 2018 report claims that Sivas graduates thought the curriculum was not relevant to their daily work and that the high-level content was misaligned with the everyday work for women police on their return to Afghanistan.[104] The language barrier was also a concern in that it reduced the quality of their learning experience.[105] An overview of the curriculum is outlined below.

Box 8.

Sivas Police Training Centre Curriculum

- Anti-corruption
- Arresting and detention (criminal principles and procedure)
- Bombs and explosives and mine awareness
- Communication skills

---

[104] WPSO and OXFAM, *Afghan Women Police*.
[105] Ibid.

- Community policing
- Computer technology
- Counter terrorism
- Crime prevention
- Crime scene investigation and evidence collection
- Criminal intelligence analysis
- Criminal investigation and other crime investigation
- Difficulties that women police officers encounter at work and sexual harassment
- Dispute resolution and mediation
- Domestic violence
- Drug addiction and narcotics
- Facility protection
- First aid
- Passport and travel documents forgery
- Human rights
- Interviews and interrogation techniques
- Juvenile policing and delinquency
- Leadership and management
- Logistics
- Official report writing
- Police case study
- Police ethics and values
- Police interrogation methods and techniques
- Radio operation
- Police duties at the police station
- Searching techniques
- Topography/map reading

- Traffic policing and driver training
- Weapons and shooting training
- Afghan jam nezam
- Afghan Police Inheritance Law
- Afghan Police Law
- Afghanistan's border neighbours
- MOIA structure, MOIA service principles
- Afghan Constitution

Police training globally comes in various forms depending on the political, historical, cultural and economic context. Police academy training does not necessarily lead to a bachelor qualification, especially in Anglo-American jurisdictions. Differences in the US and German approaches to police training following the invasion of Afghanistan demonstrate stark differences in importing training approaches (e.g., militarised, short, tactical training by the US compared to civilian-oriented, extended, theoretical training by Germany). Notwithstanding, there are many variations in police entry-level training across the globe, including across traditional and Islamic societies.

While standardisation of police training can be important for consistency among international organisations in post-conflict societies and peacekeeping operations, it can be less effective if not tailored specifically to the context and audience where it is delivered.[106] The suitability of training depends on the needs and realities of the police officers (including age, ethnicity, gender, class and ability) and the society where they serve. In this study, police trainers who served on international deployments in Afghanistan between 2006 and 2014

---

[106] Caparini, "Gender Training".

described being charged with delivering training for Afghan police that was unsuitable due to a number of assumptions embedded in the standardised curriculum which in some cases had been used in other post-conflict countries without adaptation for Afghanistan. These curriculums included assumptions relating to: learning styles, literacy and knowledge of behaviours that could or should constitute crimes according to international standards. Consequently, the design of police training should include consultation with police to better understand the training audience, and with community members to ascertain their security concerns and needs. Police training developed, designed and delivered in collaboration with local Afghan civil society organisations is more likely to be relevant and nuanced to local needs and can lay the foundations for future partnerships.[107]

Crucially, dedicated training for women police to serve in Afghanistan requires alignment between the aspirations and needs of women recruited, their training and the nature of their deployment. Misalignment of these stages can result in poor retention rates. Retention of women police, especially in the first year following graduation, was described as a serious concern during this research. Despite significant investment in training women at Sivas, data relating to whether graduates remain employed and where appears not to be available. It is not clear why this is the case; however, limited administrative and management capability within the MoIA and ANP is likely a factor. Detailed information about the status of Sivas graduates would contribute to better understanding whether the return on investment on international training is worthwhile.

---

[107] Coyne and Nyborg, "Pushing on a string?".

Short courses and upskilling

A range of in-service short courses are provided to police by international advisors and programs. In some cases, Afghan nationals who

Photo: Aurora V. Alambra / UNAMA

Image 2. The Police-e-Mardume in the ANP in Bamyan province visiting schools in 2013 in Yakawlang district to implement a safety outreach campaign aimed at helping increase public trust and confidence in their work.

have been trained as trainers under international programs carry out these courses. For women, these often target subjects such as gender-based violence, self-defence, confidence and assertiveness. Other courses include legal and computer training, first-aid, leadership and literacy. Adult learning methods such as using role plays and workshops with other health and social services practitioners are good practice and can help overcome learning challenges associated with lower levels of literacy.

Deployment and retention: women's meaningful participation in policing

Most women enter the ANP as patrol officers or non-commissioned officers and are deployed as searchers or guards. These roles have low status and officers who work in them are illiterate or have low levels of literacy among both men and women. It is estimated that between 25 and 75 per cent of women police are illiterate.[108] Even though a 2016 study found that 84.5 per cent of the female cadets surveyed in that cohort hoped to do "clerical work (office work)" after graduating from training,[109] a lack of literacy may preclude them from being able to contribute in these roles.

There has long been concern about the nature of police deployment immediately after training, including for men. In particular, initial deployments for both men and women are often as guards which means they do not use knowledge or skills gained from the training they have completed. In 2021, there are still challenges deploying women, notwithstanding the above-mentioned new policies, for many months after their training. Consequently, newly qualified women are often staying at home until they can be assigned to a position. Improving the management of this process may contribute to better retention of women police. Given the low levels of women in formal employment in general, the socialisation process for women into their workplace—especially a male-dominated one—needs to be carefully managed to build up a collective knowledge of norms and practices. Women's peer-to-peer learning and exchange of experiences and information here is imperative.

---

[108] Ministry of Interior Affairs, Women in Police Roadmap 2021–2024; WPSO and OXFAM, *Afghan Women Police*.
[109] JICA and GIWPS, *Case study on Afghanistan*, 27.

During a consultation with representatives from GIZ for this research, normalisation of seeing women in policing was highlighted as an important part of their program. For example, women police are encouraged to visit schools and share safety information with school children. The children are given notebooks with images of women police, police emergency contact numbers and safety tips to share with their parents and increase exposure of women in uniform within families.

Some women refer to fieldwork as having lower status than clerical work and that many field activities such as traffic duties are considered low-level and undesirable jobs. This may explain why only 15 per cent of the female cadets surveyed hoped to pursue field duties.[110]

Among women surveyed, 56 per cent of respondents said they 'never' perform tasks outside the scope of their work, while 36 per cent said they 'somewhat' or 'very often' do. Nine per cent of women police were required to do non-professional work, including cleaning, making tea and washing police uniforms.[111] Notwithstanding, a participant from an international agency said:

> At the moment in Afghanistan women are being assassinated for being police, judges, journalists and more. We need to be careful about what is described as 'menial' work. Some women may prefer to do administration or make tea in a safe workplace.

Indeed, in changing attitudes towards women in policing in a traditional society, women's presence in roles they are comfortable with helps to build their confidence and acceptance and demonstrate the value they bring so they can thrive. People in the community, especially women, have different needs as recipients of a policing service. Building trust and confidence, and accessing intelligence due to the

---

[110] Ibid.
[111] Ibid.

proximity women have to other women can be achieved by women police with low literacy, not wearing a uniform or carrying a gun, and not working within a confined space with a male officer.

Crucially, significant gains have been made with respect to attitudes towards women serving as police officers, with increasing acceptance among local elders and religious leaders.[112] A senior religious leader interviewed in this study said women had important roles in policing in relation to engaging with women in the community, especially in relation to searching houses where women are present and responding to victim-survivors of gender-based violence.[113]

Specialist and skills-based functions

A recurring theme among reports on the ANP and during consultations for this research is the pervasive impact of weak administration and management and a lack of implementation capability. A male participant from the MoIA said: "Men are too focused on fighting and so they don't pay attention to the administration". Another participant from the MoIA said: "They [recruiters] keep recruiting midwives [to be women police], but we need lawyers, psychologists and economic skills to fill these much-needed gaps".

In some police jurisdictions it is common to find women officers occupying office-based roles of this nature, in part because they are more amenable to balancing family responsibilities. An ANP officer said there is a one-year program at the Kabul Police Academy for people with a bachelor degree from another university to join the police in a specialist field. He indicated that the incentive structures for women police could be adapted to attract women with qualifications which would address some of the skill gaps mentioned above.

---

[112] APPRO, *Women in Afghan National Police.*

[113] Interview with religious leader (1) in December 2020.

As a result, more (qualified) women could be recruited to the police and contribute to the overall functioning of the ANP which, in turn, could improve the institutional capacity to recruit and retain more women across other ranks.

As part of recruitment campaign planning, the Gender and Human Rights Technical Working Group has included a focus on programs providing STEM (science, technology, engineering and mathematics) and medical training to women in the ANDSF, making them eligible for follow-on technical careers and training in the civilian workforce, as well as to women with information technology skills.

Photo UNAMA / Shamsuddin Hamedi.

Image 3. TAKHAR, 19 September 2018 – Local men build a police check post in Tang-e-Farkhar, Taloqan in Takhar province.

Even though safety issues may deter some women from working outside the office, they may find policing and security work more meaningful and satisfactory through other contributions. Women only constitute 3 per cent of the recruitment command,[114] although this is an area where women could make a greater contribution. For example, an interviewee said:[115]

> *A lot of women would really like to be involved in where the decision-making processes are happening. We have women at the lower ranks, but a lot of women police are not involved in direct battle ... Culturally, Afghan women will feel comfortable if they get involved in the administration aspects of policing and in the policy drafting section in relation to peace and security. I think they will feel more comfortable in that because it is acceptable to them and their families to get these positions. I don't think they will agree to work directly in combat. Even if they work in the provinces with the local government offices, they will be more comfortable doing paperwork sections.*

As the excerpt below outlines, women police in Afghanistan are aware of the gendered expectations of them and individual women may choose to exercise their agency and resistance in relation to gender norms in different ways which may be overt or subtle.[116]

Box 9.

Excerpt from Afghan Women Police: Tomorrow's force for inclusive security[117]

[Women] generally understand the cultural and traditional perspectives around their image and roles in a still conservative society but do not wish to be limited by this external context. They

---

[114] UNDP, *Policewomen Census*, 17–18.

[115] Interview with Afghan female WPS advisor in February 2020.

[116] See Amin and Alizada, "Alternative Forms of Resistance: Afghan Women Negotiating for Change", *Journal of International Women's Studies* 21, 6 (2020).

[117] WPSO and OXFAM, *Afghan Women Police*, 17.

wish to undertaken [sic] important tasks related to policy making, planning, management, administration, public outreach, strategic communication and criminal investigations, thereby gradually changing the perceptions of men and women alike.

Women comprise only 6 per cent of officers working in the police health department,[118] despite this deployment potentially being a protection measure associated with social acceptability and perceptions of women in policing, given that some women tell others they work in a hospital due to a lack of acceptance of women as police.[119] On average, two police-only hospitals exist in each province (one under the provincial chiefs of police and one clinic in the education commands) which are dedicated only to the police force. In western Kabul, there is a 200-bed hospital dedicated to police. In some police jurisdictions, health and police hospitals often have higher proportions of women officers than in other functional departments. The COVID-19 pandemic has also propelled the importance of police cooperation with the Ministry of Public Health. UNDP-LOTFA provided assistance to upgrade police hospitals in a number of provinces to be better equipped to manage the COVID-19 outbreak.[120] Moreover, police have a role in informing the community about public health protections and laws, and women police have an important role in sharing public health information with women and children in the community.

In a discussion with representatives from an international agency, concerns were raised about the way roles are designated. For example,

---

[118] UNDP, *Policewomen Census*, 17–18.

[119] See APPRO, *Women in Afghan National Police*.

[120] UNDP, "Police Equipped to Combat COVID-19 Pandemic Effectively in Northern Provinces of Afghanistan", accessed May 1, 2021, *www.af.undp.org/content/afghanistan/en/home/presscenter/pressreleases/2020/PoliceEquippedtoCombatCOVID-19inNorthernProvinces.html.*

police working in forensics have to enter at lower ranks and then progress to being assigned as forensic scientists. This means that police working in forensics can be called away to do other tasks and the pool of potential forensic officers is limited to serving police, typically men. This was seen as a missed opportunity to advance the civilianisation process of the ANP and women's inclusion. A possible solution could be to amend the incentive structure to attract women university graduates of forensic science which could secure a safer working environment for women.

Given the cultural constraints and the low FLFP among women in general, women police do not have to be at the forefront of visible frontline policing to be considered pioneering in Afghanistan. Indeed, by virtue of working at all, women may be seen as transgressing cultural and gender norms and may only be on account of extreme poverty.

At present, the most common role for women police is as searchers which indicates a generalist approach to women's deployment. It would serve the MoIA well to undertake institutional capacity and development assessments across *tashkeel* positions to identify credible roles for women and increase their representation across a wider range of departments to better reflect their capabilities, aspirations, status and safety needs.

Family response units

Specialised police services and facilities are evidence-based approaches to encouraging women victim-survivors to seek help and report gender-based violence.[121] In Afghanistan, the first family response unit

---

[121] Carrington et al., "How Women's Police Stations Empower Women, Widen Access to Justice and Prevent Gender Violence", *International Journal for Crime, Justice and Social Democracy* 9, 1 (2020); Denney, *Policing and Gender*; Natarajan and Babu, "Women Police Stations".

(FRU) was opened in 2006[122] and they now operate in all provinces. In 2018, 9 per cent of women police worked at an FRU[123] and women account for 40 per cent of all FRU officers.[124] These units contribute to strengthening institutional responses to violence against women and girls by providing safe and confidential spaces to ensure survivors of violence can report crimes in safety and dignity.[125]

> *Women go to the police station and don't see a woman officer and so don't feel comfortable to report to the men. The problem is we do not have enough female officers to take these reports and talk to these victims because female victims feel more comfortable talking to female officers and that's the problem in a lot of provinces is that we don't have enough female police officers. A lot of focus is on the capital and it is kind of understandable as well because a lot of female officers will not be feeling comfortable to be going to a province where it is fully dominated by male officers. (Youth and WPS female interviewee)*[126]

Under the Technical Advice for Improving Policing in Afghanistan (TAIPA) program, five-day specialised skills training is being provided to FRU officers in 2021. The curriculum includes: legal frameworks, basic investigation skills, victim support (psychological), preparation of prosecutor files and mediation. Importantly, the curriculum was developed using a consultative process which identified the knowledge and skill gaps that needed to be addressed. The program aims to train FRU officers from all provinces by the end of 2021, as well as deliver a train-the-trainer program.

---

[122] United Nations Population Fund, "Afghanistan's First Family Response Unit Open for Business". January 24, 2006, *www.unfpa.org/news/afghanistans-first-family-response-unit-open-business.*

[123] UNDP, *Policewomen Census*, 17–18.

[124] UNAMA, *In Search of Justice for Crimes of Violence Against Women and Girls* (UNAMA United Nations Office of the High Commissioner for Human Rights, December 2020).

[125] Ibid.

[126] Interview with Afghan female WPS advisor in February 2020.

Engaging with the health sector is essential to achieving the police mandate to prevent, detect and investigate crime. For example, the Ministry of Public Health and health care workers are needed to build legal cases to collect evidence relating to gender-based violence. Successful collection and securing of forensic evidence—especially in cases of sexual violence—is necessary to effectively prosecute crime. Building capability to work smoothly and share information between the police and health sector is also important for the effective investigation of suicide among women, particularly to better identify the causes of suicide which may be the result of violence.[127] These relationships also help to transform the policing institution to one that is more likely to retain women police in meaningful roles.

A female officer said she and her FRU colleagues often preferred not to wear uniforms outside the station because it helped them move around the community and speak to women to collect information and intelligence, or advise on medical services, psychosocial support and record statements without placing themselves and the women they speak to at risk. Therefore, as this specific example highlights, the goal of increasing visibility of women police in uniform may conflict with the operational effectiveness of FRU officers and their ability to be gender-responsive, thus necessitating a flexible uniform policy.

Officer retention

Retention of both men and women in the police has been an issue over a long period. In 2006, estimates contained in other reports refer to an attrition rate of approximately 15 per cent, possibly as high as 30 per

---

[127] Williamson, "The Role of Women in Nation-Building: Rocking the Boat at the Risk of Making It Capsize?" *Human Rights* 13, 2 (2019), https://doi.org/10.22096/hr.2019.105277.1100.

cent[128] and even higher in some specific units.[129] Some contributing factors for attrition among women were family and pressure from the local community, and among men, family pressure, a failure of the system to meet pay expectations and excessive corruption (e.g., recruits were forced to give part of their pay to higher-ranking officers).[130]

There has been an uptick of violence against women journalists, judges and activists amid peace process negotiations which may affect both recruitment and retention of women. In the first quarter of 2021, there was a 29 per cent increase in civilian casualties compared to the same quarter in 2020.[131] There was a 37 per cent increase in the number of women casualties in the same period.[132] During a meeting for this research, the head of the FRU referred to a recent attempted assassination on one of her FRU officers in which the officer's husband was killed.

Participants consulted for this research referred to challenges retaining women in the ANP (see Figure 11). Although data were not available to understand more precisely the reasons why women ceased working or major attrition points, only 13 per cent of women police said they would encourage other Afghan women to join the police.[133]

Addressing these barriers requires societal and institutional changes, as well as changes in individual attitudes and perceptions towards gender roles.

---

[128] These estimates are drawn from CSTC-A reports and interviews with students and trainers from RTCs. US Department of State and US Department of Defence, "Interagency Assessment of Afghanistan Police Training and Readiness" (November 2006), 22–25.

[129] Planty and Perito, *Police Transition*.

[130] Ibid.

[131] UNAMA, *Afghanistan Protection of Civilians in Armed Conflict: First Quarter Report 2021* (April 2021).

[132] Ibid.

[133] UNDP, *Policewomen Census*, 28.

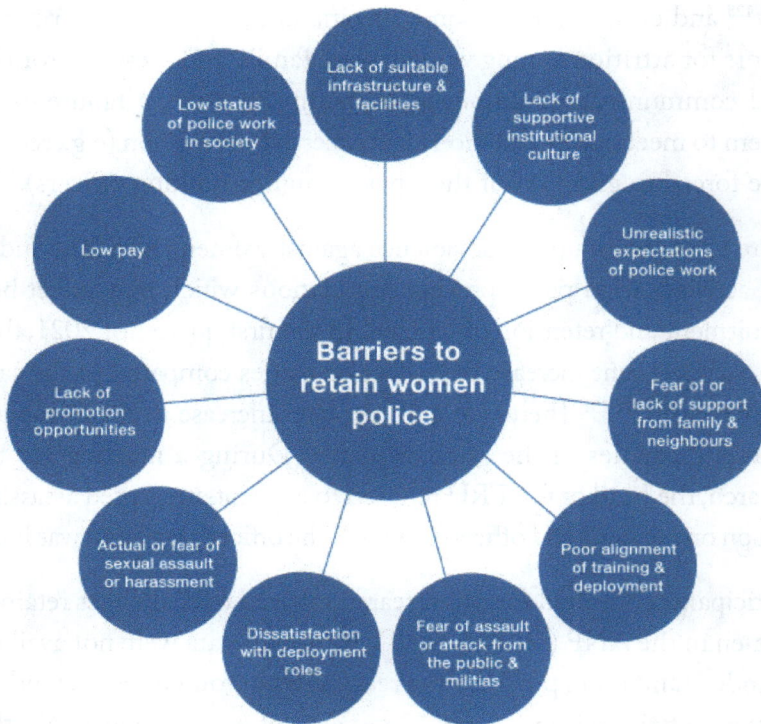

A circular diagram centered on "Barriers to retain women police" with surrounding barriers: Lack of suitable infrastructure & facilities; Low status of police work in society; Lack of supportive institutional culture; Low pay; Unrealistic expectations of police work; Lack of promotion opportunities; Fear of or lack of support from family & neighbours; Actual or fear of sexual assault or harassment; Poor alignment of training & deployment; Dissatisfaction with deployment roles; Fear of assault or attack from the public & militias.

Figure 11. Barriers to retaining women in the ANP

Developing women police, decision-making and direct entry

Globally, and especially in the Asia region, women are rarely found among senior police ranks.[134] Some police agencies are making progress towards supporting women to reach leadership levels, yet change is slow, even in countries with decades of political and social stability.[135] Consequently, developing women police to reach senior ranks in Afghanistan is a long-term project.

---

[134] INTERPOL, UN Women and UNODC, *Women in Law Enforcement*.
[135] Ibid.

The Afghanistan National Policewomen Census Survey found that 37 per cent of women police were pursuing an academic degree in 2018. Those studying were from Kabul (611), Herat (102), Balkh (60), Jowzjan (43) and Daikundi (37).[136]

The Afghanistan National Policewomen Census Survey found that 86 per cent of women police claimed to have "adequate technical and professional skills to fulfil their duties as an officer" and that 42 per cent wanted to reach a higher rank.[137] Given estimates that between 25 and 75 per cent of women police are illiterate,[138] their perception of having adequate skills may relate to current rather than future roles. Women's self-reporting of adequacy may also have been influenced by limitations on privacy when participating in the survey, thus affecting their responses.[139] Specific areas in which women wanted to receive more training include: computer training (51%), weapons training (51%), driving (51%), English (45%), literacy (43%), and management and leadership (42%).

Afghanistan's specific security environment means that considerable resources and skills are needed to address counter-insurgencies, counter-narcotics and organised crime, among others. These areas include roles that span from frontline to office-based coordination and analyst roles. In Indonesia, a majority Muslim country, women would typically begin their policing careers in gendered roles, but over time expand their capabilities across cybercrime, counter-terrorism, anti-human trafficking, narcotics investigations, criminal intelligence and financial crime investigations (see Annex 1). Women police in Indonesia enjoyed these roles because they were specialist office-based

---

[136] UNDP, *Policewomen Census*, 21.

[137] Ibid., 27.

[138] Ministry of Interior Affairs, Women in Police Roadmap 2021–2024; WPSO and OXFAM, *Afghan Women Police*.

[139] The report notes women likely completed the orally administered survey in the presence of others. UNDP, *Policewomen Census*, 11.

roles which allowed them to manage their family responsibilities. These roles enable women to be meaningfully engaged in security and policing work while not being deployed to the field alongside men or on night shifts which may not be desirable for religious or cultural reasons.

Appointing qualified women through direct entry initiatives to strategic decision-making roles in the provinces could contribute to developing effective mechanisms to deploy more women outside of Kabul.

One Afghan WPS advisor (female) remarked on the importance of governors in the provinces, that they should be the first focal point, and the possibility for new policy of appointing women as deputy governors which would be a good liaison point to do advocacy: "Deputies are working at an administrative level on policy, not combat strategies because they are also concerned about their security".[140]

Photo: UNAMA / Aurora V. Alambra.

Image 4. Members of the first ever Police Women's Committee, established with UNAMA's support in the Afghan National Police (ANP) 2011.

---

[140] Interview with Afghan female WPS advisor in February 2020.

Women role models and peer-to-peer learning

Role models are important, especially to inspire and mentor junior women who are navigating their way in new workplaces, particularly male-dominated ones. However, while mentoring can support women and help them cope at work, attention needs to focus on changing the power structures which typically expect women to meet a standard that is set by default for men.

Identifying women leaders and supporting their capacity to be role models form part of recommendations in both the Women in Police Roadmap 2021–2024 and the Women & Peace Studies Organisation and OXFAM 2018 report. The Roadmap aims to develop on-the-job training and initiate mentoring programs for women across different levels of the organisation. Importantly, this aims to include mentors from inside and outside the police.

Women role models and leaders are needed based on competencies to foster:[141]

- self-efficacy
- emotional resilience
- life-balance and energy management
- self-identification of personal leadership styles
- mentoring and coaching relationships
- the development of professional networks acting as gateways to professional advancement

Police Women's Councils (PWCs) and other informal women's peer-support associations were established in Kabul and some provinces prior to 2013. Their presence aimed to build solidarity and support between women police as they navigate their way in

---

141 Natarajan, "Gender Equality in Law Enforcement".

a challenging work environment. However, the MoIA and Gender Directorate have limited capacity to support them to be effective.[142] Although the LOTFA project indicates support for police women's councils,[143] they have largely been dormant since the end of the EUPOL Afghanistan mission in December 2016.

Underscoring the importance of funding or sponsorship for Afghan women police to expand their professional networks, a participant in this research described the importance of regional and international peer-to-peer support networks in relation to building the capability of women police as follows:[144]

> *In Afghanistan, women are not aware of what other [police] women are doing; they can share challenges. We could provide a kind of exchange with policewomen from Bangladesh and the Philippines and they can talk to Afghan women police and share their experiences and say: 'These are the problems we are facing in our countries and this is what we are doing'. This will allow Afghan officers ways to see women doing different roles in different forces. This would contribute to women doing different roles. I see women in the international police [in Afghanistan], but I don't see them talk to the women in community peacebuilding activities in an informal way and share their experiences, especially for women in the provinces. We need more women police to share their stories so more women feel more comfortable. 'This is happening to me and this is happening to you' and we can learn from each other.*

In 2014, the International Association of Women Police (IAWP) sought to support women in the ANP by advocating for their professional development. Notably, IAWP holds annual training conferences

---

[142] WPSO and OXFAM, *Afghan Women Police.*
[143] UNDP-LOTFA, project document.
[144] Interview with Afghan female WPS advisor in February 2020.

for women which include peer networking as well as skills training, knowledge building and leadership education. There are other Asia regional conferences for women police supported by IAWP or other donors and international agencies with programs relating to transnational policing and the women, peace and security agenda in which Afghan women police could participate.

Building women's networks and peer relationships in the region forms part of a four-year (2018–2022) joint initiative by the European Union (EU) and the United Nations Office on Drugs and Crime (UNODC) with implementation support from the International Organisation for Migration (IOM) and includes Afghanistan, Iran, Iraq and Pakistan.[145] The program includes developing mentoring relationships between junior and senior policewomen, domestically and bilaterally, and sharing personal experiences in policing.

Jane Townsley (Executive Director, IAWP) highlighted the importance of the quadrilateral country project for Afghan women police:

> *Semi-formal and informal approaches to peer learning and networking are essential for working women across a range of sectors, but are especially important in the security sector in Afghanistan given the small proportion of women in them.*

According to consultations with participants for this research, a particular challenge for women's peer networks in policing in Afghanistan is in relation to ethnic divisions, whereby women may be more inclined to establish networks according to ethnic lines rather than gender. Nonetheless, all women in Afghanistan have some shared experience based on their gender, and women's networks and information exchange help women to empower each other through shared experience and

---

[145] UNODC, "GLO.ACT Convenes 1st Meeting of its Women's Network Advisory Board", September 22, 2020, *www.unodc.org/unodc/en/human-trafficking/glo-act2/Countries/glo-act-convenes-1st-meeting-of-its-womens-network-advisory-board.html.*

should continue to be reinforced and encouraged. The Women in Police Roadmap 2021–2024 includes plans to bolster these networks.

The safety of women police in Afghanistan

Women who take up employment in policing can experience physical and psychological harm from the community, who may see women police as transgressing 'moral' boundaries of gender norms, as well as from male colleagues who sexually assault or exploit women at work. Women police are also at risk where they live because family members and neighbours may not only physically assault them but exclude them from important family and social networks necessary for support. An Afghan WPS advisor summed up the risk environment for women police in the following way:

> In my experience in Afghanistan, if women go to combat they will experience sexual harassment. A lot of women are not single, they are married, so administration suits them. If women are shown on social media they can receive death threats. There is a lot of organised crime, as well as their closest family members can be a threat to these women if they are seen and they can get a lot of backlash. It's not just culture, women are concerned about their security. The government doesn't have that much capacity to focus on the security of these women and that's a vicious cycle because you can't focus on one thing because so many things need to be focused on.

There appears to be varying levels of anxiety and support among women police in relation to being exposed on social media. As a result, using images of women police should be done with caution and with their permission.

Even though the Directive on Sexual Harassment 2013 and the Policy on the Prevention of Violence Against Women and Children at the

MoIA and Society Level 2013 were enacted, the lack of administrative and bureaucratic capacity of the GIRoA and the MoIA in general also affects their ability to prevent, investigate and respond to violence against women officers.[146]

The AIHRC conducted a survey to assess the nature and extent of harassment towards women working in the MoIA and MoD. The types of harassment women experienced included: verbal harassment (e.g., saying lustful words, receiving phone calls, telling jokes and sexual sarcastic words, sexual comments on appearance, dress and beauty. See Figure 12); non-verbal harassment (e.g., inappropriate and lustful looks, winking and showing inappropriate images/pictures. See Figure 13); and physical harassment (e.g., getting too close, inappropriate body touch and taking women's hands. See Figure 14).

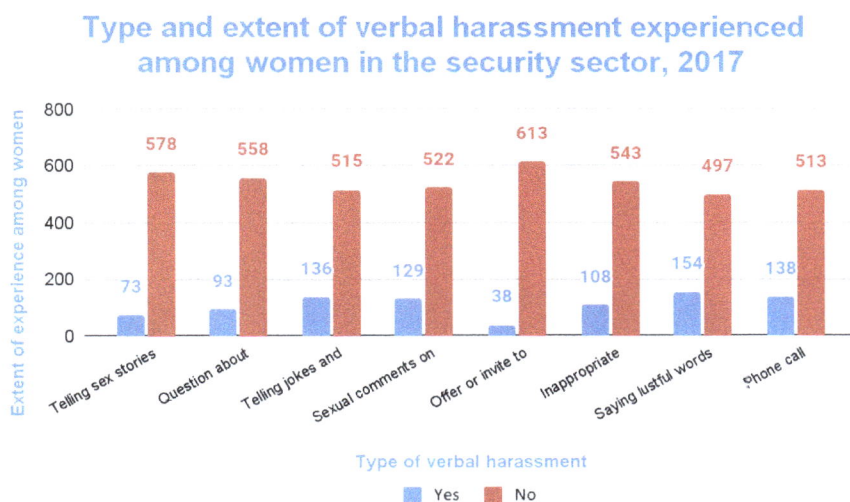

Type and extent of verbal harassment experienced among women in the security sector, 2017

Source: AIHRC, Situation of Women Employed in Defense and Security Sectors (Autumn 2017), 21–22.

Figure 12.   Type and extent of verbal harassment experienced among women in the security sector, 2017

---

146 WPSO and OXFAM, *Afghan Women Police.*

Type and extent of non-verbal harassment experience among women in the security sector, 2017

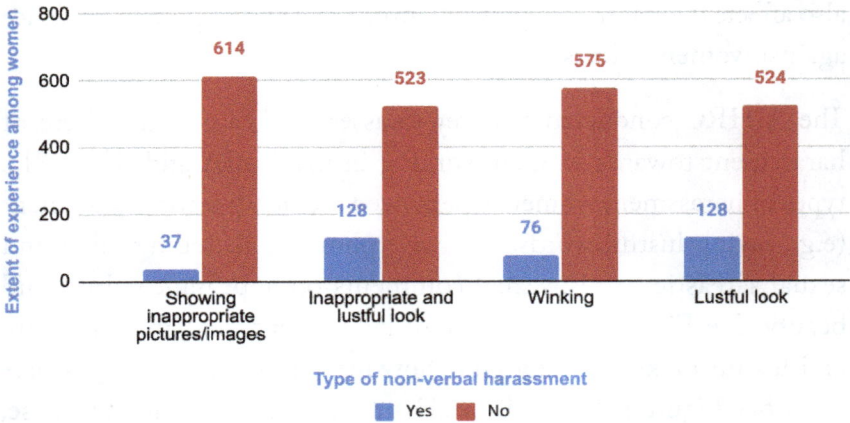

Source: AIHRC, *Situation of Women*, 22.

Figure 13. Type and extent of non-verbal harassment experience among women in the security sector, 2017

Type and extent of physical harassment experienced among women in the security sector, 2017

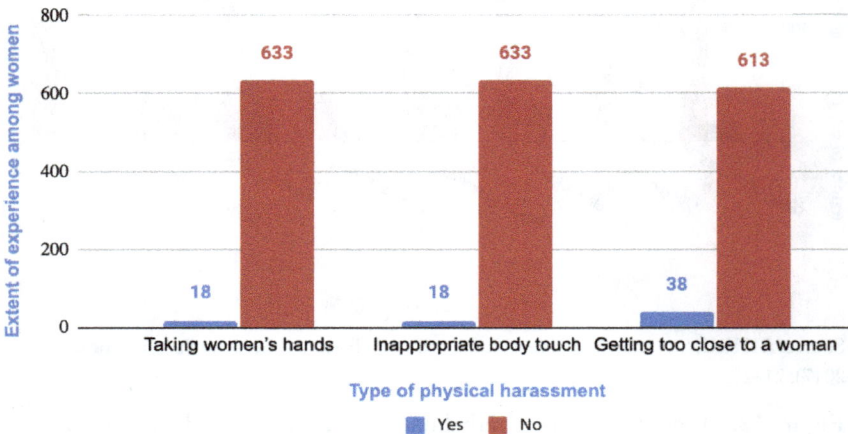

Source: AIHRC, *Situation of Women*, 23.

Figure 14. Type and extent of physical harassment experienced among women in the security sector, 2017

The AIHRC study found that 77 per cent of women who made a formal complaint to superiors said the perpetrators received a notice or warning about their behaviour, but only 2 per cent of women said their perpetrator was dismissed.[147]

The Ministry of Women Affairs (MoWA) was established to be the lead agency for promoting women's rights and advancement, however, participants in this research indicated it operated more as a case management body lacking the requisite strategic oversight and capacity building role of other government departments. In 2014, the IAWP commenced a campaign to put safeguarding systems in place to ensure women are better protected and have critical experience and resources that are available to support the ANP.

The Ombudsman Unit at the AIHRC was established as an external monitoring mechanism to ensure the defence and security forces uphold human rights in their activities and to promote transparency of accountability to the security forces.[148] The unit has responsibilities for monitoring and investigation, handling and following up complaints, and awareness raising and reporting. This is important due to concerns that perpetrators of sexual violence can often operate in Afghanistan with impunity, including perpetrators who work for security forces. In 2020, 271 cases of sexual and gender-based violence were documented by the United Nations Assistance Mission in Afghanistan (UNAMA).[149] Among these, 18 cases were verified as conflict-related sexual violence with some attributed to members of the Taliban, ANA, ANP and Afghan Local Police (ALP).[150]

---

[147] AIHRC, *Situation of Women*, 24.

[148] AIHRC, *Situation of Women*.

[149] United Nations Security Council, *Conflict-related Sexual Violence: Report of the Secretary-General*, S/2021/312 (United Nations, 2021), 8.

[150] Ibid.

The MoIA's Directorate of Gender and Human Rights and the Police-119 phone number are examples of legal mechanisms to report sexual and gender-based violence internally and the LOTFA project is currently working to improve these mechanisms. Furthermore, the ANP have established provincial and central investigative and support committees to address these behaviours, although few complaints are lodged despite widespread anecdotal reports of sexual harassment and assault within the security forces.

The lack of a competent chain of command from lower to senior ranks means that victim-survivors of sexual harassment, assault and rape at work have few trustworthy, formal mechanisms through which to report these crimes. In some cases, women police who are victim-survivors call directly to ministerial-level contacts to complain or seek to resolve an issue without a formal complaint. Reluctance to lodge a formal complaint is understandable, due to there often being heftier repercussions for complainants rather than perpetrators. During consultations for this research, gender-sensitive and confidential reporting mechanisms were described as critical to ensuring women felt comfortable their complaint would be handled appropriately, though these required increased investment and capacity building.

Gender education and training for men and women

For the foreseeable future, men will dominate the ranks of police in Afghanistan. Consequently, the education and training of men in relation to gender is essential to address harmful cultural norms that affect the treatment of both women colleagues and women in the community to make sure these relationships are respectful and supportive. The Roadmap on Women in Policing and implementation plan includes a number of initiatives in relation to training and education for both men and women in this regard, including:

- Integrating into curriculums topics of women's rights, international conventions and commitments, gender-based violence, Islam and gender, and gender-responsive policing.
- Awareness training on sexual harassment, relevant policies and reporting requirements in all police induction training and across all tiers of the organisation.
- Developing male champions to support the provision of a safe and healthy work environment for women police.
- Ensuring gender analysis is included in training relating to specialist skills courses such as investigation, anti-terrorism, security, and intelligence to enhance understanding of the security needs of women and men.

While there is training on gender, human rights and gender-based violence, there is little evidence of institutionalised training involving people with lived experience (where safe to do so) and of a wider range of thematic areas where human rights protections are operationalised. Gender training for police who may be deployed on post-conflict missions or as gender advisors has been critiqued for delivering content that is "too abstract" and difficult to relate to the context in which they work.[151] Narrative and storytelling methods are recommended training approaches to enable deeper understanding of the gendered dynamics which shape behaviour of both police (including at work and within their personal and family relationships) and people they interact with in the community.[152]

---

[151] Caparini, "Gender Training", 139.
[152] Ibid.

Photo: Rahmatullah Mazloom / UNAMA

Image 5. Training in Qala-e-Zal district of north-eastern Kunduz province by the UNAMA's human rights officers in 2014 on various aspects of Afghanistan's laws in protecting women's rights, particularly the Law on the Elimination of Violence against Women.

An important part of police learning is to engage with health and social services who provide services to vulnerable people, for example, women's refuges, and services for people who may engage in drug use or sex work as a result of trauma and precarity. When police have a better understanding of the services these organisations provide, they are more likely to be equipped with knowledge about trauma-informed policing and the importance of deflecting vulnerable people away from criminal sanctions which can embed marginalisation and poverty. Even though there is limited availability of these services in Afghanistan, police should be aware of their role in responding to these situations, and while site visits and situational engagement are important, the limited mobility of women police can make these adult learning approaches difficult in the current security context.

Women-oriented working conditions

Maternity and parental leave

Article 54 of the Labor Law 2007 provides an entitlement of 90 days maternity leave. While paternity leave is not explicit, Article 51(3) of the Labor Law 2007 stipulates:

Employees are entitled to (10) days of urgent leave for marriage; death of father, mother, brother, sister, spouse, child, father in-law, mother in-law, uncle, aunt; or birth of a baby.

It was reported that male police officers do not use their entitlement although it is unclear if this is because they are unaware of their entitlement or because it is part of the occupational culture or practice that acts as a disincentive for its uptake.[153]

Family-oriented work hours

According to a recent study, 62 per cent of women police are married and 70 per cent have children.[154] Family responsibilities are common reasons why women prefer to do office-based police work as it is more conducive to balancing work and home life. While women may believe they are capable of duties in the field, research in other jurisdictions has found that office work is a pragmatic way women can combine a policing career with having a family.[155]

The Labor Law 2007 does not provide provisions to support part-time or flexible work, although during consultations for this research it appears the ANP makes accommodations to help women manage their formal and informal work.

---

[153] Personal communication with a female employee of an international agency in 2021.

[154] UNDP, *Policewomen Census*, 4.

[155] INTERPOL, UN Women and UNODC, *Women in Law Enforcement*.

According to Article 121 of the Labor Law 2007:

> *It shall not be permissible for women and youth to be employed in night work. However, women and nursing mothers may be employed as night workers in accordance with the work schedule and in rotation in hospitals, health clinics, and, subject to their agreement, in duties where there is an urgent need.*

Notwithstanding, accommodations may be made and the MoIA pays an 'Operative and night shift duty incentive'.[156]

Infrastructure, facilities and equipment

The scope of this research sought to go beyond infrastructure and facilities in assessing structural barriers to women's inclusion in the ANP. Nonetheless, there has been significant investment into building barracks, changing rooms, bathrooms, day care facilities, classrooms, searching rooms and compounds for women police to reduce a lack of infrastructure and facilities as barriers for women's participation in policing.[157] In some cases, participants reported that a lack of women to utilise the facilities meant they were overtaken by men's use, and that there are difficulties in regaining these spaces for their intended purpose. Indeed, in March 2021, a Women's Police Town in Kabul was inaugurated, an area for secure housing for women police and their families, or widows of ANP officers.

As outlined earlier, gender segregated training institutions are deemed important by women police for attracting more women to the ANP because they enable women to reconcile their Islamic faith with a police career.

---

[156] Ministry of Interior Affairs, Incentives Code (2018).

[157] See, e.g., US Department of Defence, *Enhancing Security and Stability in Afghanistan* (December 2018), 98, *https://media.defense.gov/2018/Dec/20/2002075158/-1/-1/1/1225-REPORT-DECEMBER-2018.PDF.*

Creating the conditions for effective gendered reforms in the Afghan National Police

The ANP has been described as "corrupt, badly trained, and [having] a drug problem",[158] a reputation that likely contributes to challenges of attracting women to the occupation. Even though civilian and community-oriented policing are an aim for the ANP, there is a persistent pull towards combat and a reactive posture, especially in 2021 amid the withdrawal of foreign forces. Notwithstanding the potential for a deteriorating security environment, there is scope to shape an occupational culture that is more conducive to gendered reforms.

During interviews with representatives from the MoIA, MoWA, AIHRC, current and former local and international policing, gender and WPS advisors, a range of suggestions were described that could contribute to creating the conditions for sustainable gender-sensitive reform which are outlined in three categories below.

---

[158] A general of NATO's International Security Assistance Force (ASAF), quoted in Friesendorf, "Insurgency and Civilian Policing", 337.

Projecting a civilian policing image and better reflecting the range of women's roles in policing

The security situation in Afghanistan has drawn an asymmetrical focus on combat, enforcement and tactics. Images that depict militarised and tactical security functions over the relational and partnership building aspects of policing can entrench masculine stereotypes and deter women and their families from seeing the diversity of roles within police work.[159] Depictions of women police that better reflect the roles or nature of work that they are more likely to do can contribute to improving recruitment and retention rates, especially given that family and community perceptions of women are influential in whether they pursue a policing career.[160] Essentialising women may be seen to conflict with UN universalist goals for gender equality; however, prominent scholars on women in policing argue that it may not only be necessary to make progress, but that it is a culturally appropriate and gender-sensitive approach to do so.[161] Nonetheless, police-gender advisors must be cognisant of the diversity and variation among women in Afghanistan and accommodate these through multiple career pathways to cater to their needs, preferences and aspirations.

A participant from the MoIA said the ANP needs a communications strategy that projects a civilian and community-oriented, rather than militaristic, image of policing to enhance the legitimacy of the ANP. Specifically, he emphasised that ANP communications should shift away from publishing militarised images of police with firearms (both men and women) and towards depictions that reflect their civilian role

---

[159] Denney, *Policing and Gender*.

[160] Natarajan, "Police Culture and the Integration of Woman Officers in India", *International Journal of Police Science and Management* 16, 2 (2014); JICA and GIWPS, *Case study on Afghanistan*, 21.

[161] Natarajan, *Women Police*; Strobl, "Towards a 'Women-Oriented' Approach".

in the community. When asked why official communications favour sharing images of police with firearms, he said:

Some policemen like to think they look tough posing with guns. They think they are in Hollywood or something … The police also want to look strong to any attackers, but this is not the image we need to build trust with the community.

Photo: Fezeh Hosseini (UNDP)

Image 6. A police photo exhibition, "Enhancing Security and Rule of Law for Afghans," was opened on 8 June (2010) at the Kabul Serena Hotel.

An observation of publications on women police also shows a tendency to use images of them using or posing with firearms in a militarised style. Imagery of this kind can be useful for breaking down gender stereotypes and opening up opportunities for women to pursue non-traditional gender roles through promoting "collective agency".[162]

---

[162] Connell, "Accountable Conduct: 'Doing Gender' in Transsexual and Political Retrospect", *Gender & Society* 23, 1 (February 2009): 109, *https://doi.org/10.1177/0891243208327175*.

However, the extent of insecurity and the personal preferences among women police mean they are rarely deployed to or undertake roles outside the police station (in uniform) or that require firearms use. For example, women in the Afghan Border Police (ABP) informed their GPPT trainers that the nature of their deployment in Immigration and the Security Aviation Section does not require them to carry firearms.[163]

A participant from the MoIA asserted that among both official communications and external reporting and commentary, there was not enough acknowledgement of good police work and that there was little attention paid to the social work, educational, policy development and community engagement roles of police. These roles are where women police in other jurisdictions with strong traditional and patriarchal gender norms typically excel and express pride in performing.[164] Depicting women in these roles in official communications and recruitment campaigns is likely to contribute to improving public perceptions towards women in policing.

During discussions with international policing and gender advisors in Kabul, low morale and lack of a professional calling for a career in policing were identified as making recruiting and retaining police officers difficult. Official MoIA and ANP communications have an important role in not only acknowledging and reinforcing good police work, but also in developing, projecting and instilling an occupational identity that motivates officers to support, serve and protect the community. Instilling a sense of pride in ANP officers may also moderate corrupt practices by increasing adherence to professional ethics.[165]

---

[163] Personal communication with GPPT trainer in April 2021.

[164] Natarajan, *Women Police*.

[165] Singh, *Investigating Corruption in the Afghan Police Force: Instability and Insecurity in Post-Conflict Societies* (Bristol: Policy Press, 2020).

Policing, partnerships and people-centred institution building

People-centred institution building engages with non-security sector actors who act as a force multiplier by harnessing the skills and abilities of other agencies that are necessary for human security,[166] and is especially important for women's security. Engagement with non-security sector actors also contributes to building accountability mechanisms for policing in general, and as they relate to women's rights. The relational aspects of people-centred police building help develop an overall institutional culture that is conducive to women's inclusion and is relevant given a lack of a supportive institutional culture has been identified as a key challenge for gender-sensitive reform in the ANP.[167]

Participants in this study from the MoIA indicated the importance of investing in partnerships with community organisations, religious groups, mosques, schools, universities, health and social services, sporting groups, CSOs, among others. This was designated as important because it would enhance police awareness of issues in the community, increase understanding of the role of other organisations in public safety and increase accountability to the community. Indeed, the Police-e-Mardume (PeM community police) were established to work towards building closer relationships with community groups and external stakeholders.[168] However, some police say they are not well equipped to engage in activities such as community forums, and are not confident to chair or participate in meetings that require facilitation, setting an agenda and minute-taking skills.[169]

---

[166] Denney, *Policing and Gender*; Coyne and Nyborg, "Pushing on a string?".

[167] WPSO and OXFAM, *Afghan Women Police*.

[168] Ministry of Interior Affairs, "First National Police-e-Mardume Conference: Summary of Proceedings" (Kabul, Afghanistan: June 25, 2013), *https://ipcb.files.wordpress. com/2013/08/eupol-community-policing-report-july-20131.pdf*.

[169] Interview with a female international community-oriented policing specialist in January 2021.

Photo: UNAMA / Sayed Barez

Image 7. International Women's Day celebration in Mazar-i-Sharif, Afghanistan: 7 March 2013

Deliberate investment and valuing engagement with other stakeholders holds systems together in ways that may not be immediately obvious.[170] Focusing on relationships, partnerships and building social capital in policing with external agencies is important because civilian policing is not only about law enforcement, crime prevention and control, dispute resolution and access to justice, but also problem-solving, mediation, making referrals to other services, suicide investigation and prevention, mental health crises, problematic drug use and locating missing persons.[171]

---

[170] Herrington and Roberts, "Policing in Complexity: Leadership Lessons from an Annus Horribilis", *Police Chief Online*, February 10, 2021.

[171] Denney, *Policing and Gender*; Sreekumaran et al., *"Gender-responsive Policing" Initiatives Designed to Enhance Confidence, Satisfaction in Policing Services and Reduce Risk of Violence Against Women in Low and Middle Income Countries – a Systematic Review: Implications of Evidence for South Asia* (London: EPPI-Centre, Social Science Research Unit, UCL Institute of Education, University College London, December 2017).

Box 10.

The intersection of community policing and gender-sensitive reform

In policing, a turn to the community is more likely than a turn to gender in terms of worldwide police reform efforts. However, the latter turn is contained in the former. Community policing charges police with understanding the social problems of diverse peoples, working with the influence of stereotypes on decision-making, incorporating the protection of human rights and developing human resource capacity to diffuse conflicts rather than merely react to them.[172]

One MoIA participant said that he was unaware of any requirement for police district commanders in Kabul to visit or engage with any group external to the ANP. He suggested that police district commanders should have as one of their performance measures, a minimum number of regular community or multi-agency engagements per month, and that this should be mandated by MoIA leadership. Staff from the GIZ community policing program said they are exploring how to increase interaction between the police and alternative dispute resolution processes, for example, local *shuras* (e.g., community forums with elders, typically male dominated), as well as work towards increasing women's participation in *shuras*.

While the ANP needs to develop partnership policing capability as a whole, the Handbook on Gender-Responsive Police Services (2021) emphasises the importance of establishing working relationships with external stakeholders such as women's or civil society organisations,

---

[172] Strobl, "Towards a 'Women-Oriented' Approach", 97.

academia,[173] marginalised and vulnerable groups, and other key actors for a more informed response to preventing and investigating violence against women and girls.[174]

'Post'-conflict policing and officer wellbeing

The National Mental Health Strategy 2019–2023 details the impact of war in Afghanistan on the community with a nationwide study indicating that the population has consistently high levels of mental distress (26% with impairment and 46% without impairment).[175] Nonetheless, mental health literacy in Afghanistan is low and services are estimated to reach only 10 per cent of the population.[176]

Training and psychological support for women officers has gained more attention from donors than men, especially as it relates to the risks they face at work such as being exposed to women victim-survivors of gender-based violence and encountering assault or harassment from colleagues. In a survey of female police recruits, 48.8 per cent of respondents reported having experienced physical or sexual violence and the report recommends the provision of professional and culturally appropriate psychological support.[177]

The impact of trauma or mental ill-health of male police in relation to their ability to learn and perform their jobs well is not well recognised

---

[173] As an example, the Indonesia National Police and Airlangga University in Surabaya partnered to launch the Center for Women's Empowerment in Law Enforcement in 2021.

[174] UN Women, UNODC and the International Association of Women Police, *Handbook on Gender-responsive Police Services for Women and Girls Subject to Violence* (2021), 31.

[175] Ministry of Public Health, *National Mental Health Strategy 2019–2023*, 5.

[176] Human Rights Watch, "Afghanistan: Little Help for Conflict-Linked Trauma" (October 7, 2019), *www.hrw.org/news/2019/10/07/afghanistan-little-help-conflict-linked-trauma*.

[177] JICA and GIWPS. *Case study on Afghanistan*, 35.

in most accounts of reform. In this research, a former deputy head of the International Police Coordination Board (IPCB) said: "In my work in helping to build the police in Afghanistan, not one dollar from donors went towards supporting the mental health and wellbeing of police officers".[178]

In consultations for this research with the MoIA, psychological support and counselling for men was identified as something that could contribute to changing men's behaviour towards women. Recognising the pervasive psychological impacts of prolonged exposure to conflict on men,[179] especially given they are more likely to be engaged in combat or crime scenes, creates space for officer support programs that would benefit the wellbeing of both men and women. Importantly, prioritising officer wellbeing could contribute to attracting more people to the occupation, reassure families that officer welfare is supported through access to health care and help retain officers for longer.

Poor mental health and post-traumatic stress disorder (PTSD) among police were also described as barriers to building better relationships with the community because it could contribute to poor behaviours and misconduct, particularly among men, and this increases distrust between police and community members. An interviewee said that local police can "snap so quickly" and "get into a fight without even asking a [vehicle] passenger what's happening" (Afghan WPS advisor, female). While it is unclear that these actions observed by the interviewee are directly attributed to poor mental health, given the protracted conflict and insecurity, it is likely that some police could benefit from health and social support. She added:

---

[178] Personal communication with Grant Edwards, former Deputy Head, IPCB (2012–2013), in April 2021.

[179] Ministry of Public Health, *Mental Health Strategy 2019–2023*.

Police have trauma in their past lives. While mental health counselling for police is important, they also need the right counselling on how to talk, engage and interact with the community and on ethics.

Box 11 provides an excerpt from reportage on crime scene investigators in Kabul detailing the psychological toll of police work.[180]

Box 11.

"It's a very dangerous and difficult job. Honestly, I think it is having a really negative impact on my mental state. I've personally visited around 5,000 crime scenes. Homicides are just one kind of case. We see a lot of suicide cases, and also the aftermath of suicide bombings ... Here they are just photos, but I remember what it feels like to collect the flesh of someone's body in my hands and put it in a bag." (Crime Scene Investigator 1, male, Kabul)

"There is no mental health support to address the emotional toll from the work. And because of the bad security situation in our job the physical and psychological stress and side effects feel like a severe disability like deafness and blindness." (Crime Scene Investigator 2, male, Kabul)

---

[180] Billing, "A Day on the Job With Kabul's Crime Scene Investigators", Aljazeera, February 1, 2021, www.aljazeera.com/features/2021/2/1/in-afghanistan-a-day-on-the-job-with-kabuls-crime-scene-investi.

Photo: Rahmatullah Mazloom / UNAMA

Image 8. Training in Qala-e-Zal district of north-eastern Kunduz province by the UNAMA's human rights officers in 2014 on various aspects of Afghanistan's laws in protecting women's rights, particularly the Law on the Elimination of Violence against Women.

An Afghan woman working in WPS sector considered psychological support for both men and women important:

> *The first step is to talk to them and say "Ok, we have these problems" and then ask them what types of problems they are facing ... A lot of police officers have PTSD and they have different traumas in Afghanistan ... But, these issues affect their work in the police and army as well. I don't think there's been a lot of mental counselling workshops or seminars for police ... But, I think we should focus on that as well, because there are a lot of people who read reports on violence and these sorts of things and this would be a very good*

thing to do. It might be hard in the beginning because police don't talk until after a few sessions or meetings. We had this problem with police officers, they don't really talk. It takes time, but we should consider it.

Recognising that officers are part of the community with their own health, safety and security needs will contribute to building their capacity to recognise these concerns among their colleagues of any gender as well as in the communities they are meant to serve. Training and support for men is an opportunity for men to reflect on how stress (related to work, conflict, abuse, social expectations, violence etc.) influences how they experience life in Afghanistan as men and in their multiple roles as police, fathers, sons, husbands, brothers and friends. The perspectives of younger male officers are also important because they may have more exposure to variations in gender norms and understand women's plights.

Conclusion: Women in the future Afghan National Police

Afghanistan is not alone in having low representation of women in the security sector and policing. It remains a global challenge to include women into organisations that often emerged without women at all due to gendered expectations of men's and women's roles in formal and informal (especially domestic) work. Nonetheless, gender-responsive policing in Afghanistan must consider the local context, not only as it relates to culture and gender, but also the current nature of the police organisation, and the presence of armed conflict, terrorism, organised crime, drug trafficking and corruption, among others.

While it is unclear what the security situation will be in Afghanistan post-2021, women have an important contribution to make in strengthening the overall functioning of the MoIA and ANP. The MoIA, ANP and international community must enhance coordination mechanisms across all 34 provinces to enable provinces to effectively communicate with Kabul and vice versa. This complex task requires drawing on the diverse experiences and knowledge of men and women. The US has indicated it will continue to provide support to the security sector, though this is likely to be from outside Afghanistan. To date there has not been explicit commitments from the US to reorient efforts towards creating a more civilian-oriented police force, thus, prospects for de-militarisation of the ANP may be slim.

Theoretical models developed in relation to women in policing from other traditional and Islamic societies offer useful insights for elevating the status of women police in Afghanistan.[181] Gendered policing models emphasise the importance of cultural context and socially-constructed gender norms in relation to strategies to advance women's inclusion and retention. However, gendered policing models, which draw attention to gender difference, may sit uncomfortably with the UN's gender equality framework.[182] Yet, disregard for gender norms, and a focus on equality rather than equity, such as expecting women to meet the same standards as men in terms of physical tasks, shift work and operational police functions, contributes to poor retention rates among women, increased stress due to the dual burden of formal and informal work and job dissatisfaction. While women can have a transformational role in improving police institutions, they should not be expected to completely transform gender relations.[183] The latter relies more on changes in the wider society in which policing is embedded. Consequently, improving societal attitudes towards women and empowering more young men to challenge harmful social norms, including harmful masculinities, is important for the wellbeing of future generations. This will contribute to reducing gender inequality by moderating expectations of gendered behaviours for men and women.

This study aimed to provide an overview of the current status and representation of women in the ANP, reflect on lessons learned from past initiatives, identify strategies for gender-responsive police reform and identify ways to improve the physical and psychological safety of women police. Due to time and logistical restrictions, there are limitations to the scope of analysis and access to primary and secondary

---

[181] Natarajan, *Women Police* and "Police Culture"; Strobl, "Progressive or Neo-Traditional?" and "Towards a 'Women-Oriented' Approach".

[182] Strobl, "Towards a 'Women-Oriented' Approach".

[183] Ibid.

data, especially outside Kabul. While there is much appreciation for the generous time given by police and gender advisors, the study lacks insight into the status of the overall strategic, organisational change management processes that are in train and the high-level political challenges associated with this work and the success of gendered reforms intertwined with these projects.

Empirical research shows that security institutions that are civilianised, community-oriented and engaged in partnership policing are more effective in recruiting and retaining women. Thus, investment is essential to achieving much-needed collaboration and coordination between these reform projects. A focus on gender equity as a pathway to gender equality is also likely to provide ballast to progress made to date in relation to advancing women's inclusion in the security sector in Afghanistan. Crucially, the pace of change to advance gender equity and gender equality should be measured not just in years but in decades and generations.

Annexes

Annex 1: Women police in traditional and Islamic societies

Decades of research on women in policing, especially in the past two decades, have shed light on the social, cultural, occupational and institutional diversities present in policing. While there are variations in the precise model of women's inclusion, the progression model typically starts from a position of essentialising women[184] (i.e., emphasising women's differences to men and their particular gendered value to the policing mandate). However, this pathway can be seen as contrary to the United Nations' goals regarding gender equality.[185] Table 2 provides a summary of some approaches to women's participation in policing, although they are not necessarily fixed or rigid categories and more than one can function at a particular time or at different career stages. Generalist, integrated and universal approaches are more likely to be found in societies that are regarded as economically developed and with lower levels of gender inequality whereas confined, segregated and specialised approaches are more common in societies with higher levels of gender inequality and more traditional gender norms.

---

[184] Natarajan, "Domestic Violence, Culture and Justice for Women", in *Family Conversations: Let's Tell the Secrets, ed.* E. R. Rocha (Addis Ababa, Ethiopia: Henrich Boll Foundation, 2007) and "Police Culture"; Strobl "Towards a 'Women-Oriented' Approach".

[185] Ibid.

Table 2. Summary of approaches regarding women's participation in policing

Approach/model	Summary
Confined (office-based)	Refers to officer deployment where women are typically working in office-based roles, which may or may not be as a result of policy, but significantly influenced by cultural norms and practices about gendered roles in society.
Generalist	Refers to training and deployment models that provide recruits with general training for patrol or frontline work (often found in Anglo-American policing models with relatively short training, e.g., 3–12 months).
Integrated or universal	Refers to models where male and female police are recruited in similar ways, trained in the same classes or using the same curriculum and deployed to similar functions. There are typically standardised recruitment, selection and promotion criteria, though there may be some minor differences in physical criteria, e.g., strength-based assessments.
Segregated	Refers to models that segregate men and women in recruitment, training and/or deployment in accordance usually with written policies (often found in traditional or Islamic societies). The extent or consistency of segregation may vary across different roles, ranks and functions.
Specialist	Refers to recruitment, training or deployment approaches that focus on developing or attaining a particular specialised skill set. For example, some police curricula may allow recruits to specialise in administration, forensics or criminal investigations. Or graduates from other institutions may be employed for specific positions (police hospitals, women and children's units, media departments, cybercrime, forensics, legal advisors, foreign relations etc.).

A study of women police across the member states of the Association of South East Asian Nations (ASEAN) found that most countries have a maximum quota for the annual recruitment of women, typically between 10 and 20 per cent.[186] In many cases these quotas act as a ceiling on women's recruitment because there are often more applicants than positions available for women. A consistent feature among the police forces in ASEAN is that women typically perform gendered roles that are segregated, specialised and confined (e.g., office-based). Although women may have access to operational roles to varying degrees, many women reported preferring gendered or office-based roles because it enabled them more flexibility within a rigid paramilitary system to manage their home and family responsibilities.[187] More broadly, police forces with higher levels of civilian positions and part-time or flexible work generally have higher levels of women's participation.[188]

The nature of policing in a particular place is shaped by how police institutions emerged and the political, historical, economic, legal, cultural and social influences in the environment. These influences can affect whether integrated or gendered policing models are politically feasible, culturally appropriate and gender-responsive (see Table 3).

---

[186] INTERPOL, UN Women and UNODC, *Women in Law Enforcement*.

[187] Ibid.

[188] See, e.g., Institute for Public Security of Catalonia, *Women in Police Services in the EU: Facts and Figures 2012* (February 2013)

www.recercat.cat/bitstream/handle/2072/207935/WOMEN%20IN%20POLICE%20 SERVICES%20EU_2012.pdf.

Table 3. Comparison of integrated and gendered policing models in terms of policing style and the status and self-image of women officers[189]

Themes	Integrated Policing		Gendered Policing	
Policing style	1	Concentrated on patrolling	1	Diversified police response
	2	Victim assistance as a secondary responsibility	2	Better service for women victims
	3	Consistent with traditional police	3	Helpful in advancing community policing
	4	Little attention to public attitudes to police	4	Improved public attitudes to police
	5	Performance standards based primarily on strength and agility	5	Other skills valued and rewarded
Status of Women Police	1	Men and women considered equal and do the same duties	1	Men and women considered equal but do different duties
	2	Male domination	2	Gender-neutral/balanced
	3	Under-representation of women	3	Improved representation of women
	4	Under-utilisation of women's skills	4	Proper utilisation of women's skills
	5	Longer route to equality	5	Back door to equality
	6	Well suited to societies where women have equal power in all walks of life	6	Well suited to societies where women are still subordinate
Self-Image	1	Persistent dilemmas about women's abilities breed uncertainty about policing as a career	1	Empowers and strengthens women's abilities and thus reinforces determination to make policing a career
	2	Uncertainties about job security	2	Development of job security
	3	Accommodates women who are already fully emancipated	3	Accommodates women of all personalities and backgrounds
	4	Provides no clear direction concerning the unique contribution of women police	4	Sends a clear signal about the special role and competencies of women
	5	Constant need to prove themselves	5	Improves self-esteem
	6	Hard to raise voice	6	Helps to raise voice

---

[189] Natarajan, *Women Police*, 163

Retaining women in policing can be difficult even in countries considered 'developed' such as Australia, where women reported desiring equal opportunities alongside male officers in the early stages of their career, but some later preferred an office-based or non-operational role in order to manage family and caring responsibilities.[190] To counter officer attrition, especially women, police forces in Australia have adopted strategies regarding more flexibility around work hours, part-time roles and parental leave for *all* officers, alongside strong mechanisms to address sexual harassment and gender discrimination.[191]

Indonesia is a majority Muslim nation which initially segregated men and women police. The national police were absorbed into the armed forces in 1961, though regained civilian status as a separate entity in 1999 after periods of political crises and conflict. Box 12 outlines some features of reform and their implications for gender-responsive policing.

Box 12.

Women in the Indonesian National Police

The Indonesian National Police launched its Grand Strategy 2005–2025 which set out three key phases for reform: trust building (2005–10); partnerships (2010–15); and striving for excellence (2015–25). Even though it does not specifically refer to the role of women in policing, its key phases are essential for creating conditions to advance women's inclusion.

Indonesia's dominant approaches to include women in policing are a combination of segregated, specialist and confined.[192] The

---

[190] Chan et al., "Doing and Undoing Gender in Policing", *Theoretical Criminology* 14, 4 (2010), doi:10.1177/1362480610376408.

[191] VEOHRC, *Independent Review*.

[192] UN Women and UNODC, *Women in Law Enforcement in the ASEAN Region: Focus on Indonesia* (unpublished, 2021).

initial training is segregated by gender, but women can now participate in leadership training alongside men at the main academy which trains future leaders. Women can join the police after graduating from an external university with a specialist qualification. And while most women perform office-based work (confined), they do so across a range of capabilities, including: administration, cybercrime, international relations, narcotics, training, road traffic policing, airport police, forensics and disaster victim identification, counter-terrorism, anti-human trafficking, criminal intelligence, financial crime investigations. When women join at the commissioned officer level, they do not necessarily have to perform patrol work and can be assigned to a department in a specialist or office-based role.

Even though women comprise only 6 per cent of police officers in Indonesia, there are few reported concerns regarding retention of female officers.[193] Women can join the police through commissioned or non-commissioned officer pathways. The low numbers of women annually recruited outside major campaigns is less than 10 per cent which likely contributes to the low representation of women police. Nonetheless, women are making their way up the ranks and comprise approximately 10–15 per cent of middle-management commissioned officer ranks.[194]

To improve the police responses to crimes against women and girls, the Jakarta Metropolitan Police established police women's desks (RKP) at nine police stations in 1999.[195] Retired women officers became approved trainers and mentors for serving female

---

[193] INTERPOL, UN Women and UNODC, *Women in Law Enforcement*.
[194] Personal communication with Indonesia National Police officer in 2020.
[195] Harsono, "The Development of Women and Children Service Unit within the Police – the Indonesian Experience" (presentation, 2nd International Islamic Women's Conference, Islamabad, Pakistan, November 21–24, 2011), https://www.slideserve. com/jag/dr-i-rawati-h-arsono.

officers, and to act as a bridge to build relationships between the police women's desks and other community-based support services for women and child victims. These policing functions now have legal standing in decrees made by the chief of police.

To staff the units and to supplement the low levels of women police, the Indonesian National Police have used targeted campaigns, as described by a high-ranking female officer below:[196]

> *In 2013, there was a mass recruitment of 7,000 women. Because of a lack of representation of police women over the country, the government decided to recruit more women. In 2013, the percentage of female police officers was only 3.5 per cent. The President at the time wanted to increase the number so now we have 5 per cent. The plan is to deploy women police officers all over Indonesia ... In 2015 there were an additional 5,000 women recruited so that at least two women are deployed in each police station. The police station is the frontline of the police so this is why we needed to recruit more women.*

One of the drawbacks of Indonesia's approach is that even though many women enjoy their specialist or office-based roles within functional departments, they do limit their ability to transfer to other operational roles later which, in turn, limits their prospects for promotion given the weight operational experience is often given to senior ranks.[197]

Natarajan's theoretical framework on gendered policing resembles the progress of women's inclusion in policing in Indonesia. While large numbers of women may have been recruited for gendered roles, this process also allows the institution (i.e., men) to appreciate women's

---

[196] INTERPOL, UN Women and UNODC, *Women in Law Enforcement*, 61.
[197] Ibid.

contribution and adapt to changing staff composition. Evidently, the breadth of roles outlined in Box 12 demonstrates women now have access to working across a range of functions. In 2021, the Indonesia National Police and Airlangga University in Surabaya partnered together to launch a Center for Women's Empowerment in Law Enforcement to further advance women's role in policing. Change may be slow, but a gender equity model can be a pathway to gender equality in policing and can limit men's resistance to women joining the occupation.

Annex 2: Duties and obligations of ANP

Afghan Police Law 2005, Duties and Obligations, Article Five

The police shall be obliged to execute the following duties:

1   ensure and maintain public order and security;
2   ensure individual and societal security and protect their legal rights and freedoms;
3   take preventive actions to stop crimes from happening;
4   timely discover the crimes and arrest the suspects and perpetrators according to the provisions of the law;
5   counter moral deviations, in moral social behaviour and actions that disturb public tranquillity;
6   protect the properties and assets of the public and private sector as well as those of the domestic and foreign and international institutions and organisations;
7   fight against the cultivation of poppies and marijuana, smuggling and drug trafficking, production, import and consumption of intoxicants, and for their prevention;
8   fight against organised crimes and terrorism according to the provisions of the law;

9   cooperate with administrative offices in executing their jobs within their competence according to the provisions of the law;

10 regulate road traffic according to the provisions of the law;

11 take steps and necessary measures to fight against unpredictable events and circumstances;

12 help and assist victims of unpredictable events and natural disasters, rescuing them and saving their properties;

13 take steps and measures necessary in a state of emergency in order to ensure public order and security according to the provisions of the law;

14 attract public cooperation in the preventative and ad hoc operations;

15 safeguard and watch the borders;

16 control persons in the incoming and outgoing checkpoints on borders and at international airports of Afghanistan according to the provisions of the law;

17 prevent smuggling of goods;

18 take appropriate and necessary measures during the occurrence of any movements on borders which are against the national sovereignty;

19 watch border traffic and control the corresponding documents;

20 maintain cooperation and contact with border police of the neighbouring nations in accordance with the international treaties;

21 maintain cooperation and contact with the police of the foreign countries in accordance with the rules of Interpol.

Annex 3: Recommendations for reform (early 2021)

The recommendations outlined below were developed in early 2021 and are included here to be informative for others who may be working in relation to gender-sensitive police reform in other contexts.

The Women in Police Roadmap 2021–2024 (and implementation plan) and the report by the Women & Peace Studies Organisation and OXFAM 2018 provide sound recommendations for advancing gender inclusive security sector reform; however, greater attention should be paid to gender equity to better reflect the expressed preferences of women police.

The recommendations outlined below are not exhaustive and largely focus on strategic and structural interventions that aim to create an enabling environment and are important for gendered reforms to gain traction. These recommendations pertain to the work of the Afghan government, MoIA, ANP, international agencies, donors, and other non-government and civil society organisations.

Strategic-level recommendations

Structural

- **Build and augment** national capacity to train women police officers.
- **Increase** investment and prioritisation of civilianisation and community-oriented policing to reduce the asymmetrical focus on militarisation. Ensure strategic planning reflects these priorities with appropriate budget allocation for their implementation.
- **Review** performance and incentive structures, and take corresponding actions to reflect the importance of building police-community partnerships to achieve security and safety.

- **Commit** to ongoing review of the *tashkeel*[198] using a gender equity lens, with consultations between the MoIA, local and international gender advisers (where available), women police and civil society groups to accommodate women officers and better serve wider community needs in a changing security environment.

- **Enhance** the services available for supporting the welfare of all officers, e.g., access to health care, trauma treatment, psychosocial support, drug treatment, etc.

Professional support

- **Ensure** that international police gender advisers recruited are equipped with strategic knowledge regarding police reform and gendered models of policing, and are familiar of the intersection of community-oriented and partnership policing with gender-responsive reform.

- **Draw on** the expertise of police gender advisers with Islamic socio-cultural backgrounds and encourage South-to-South collaboration, advisory and exchange.

- **Increase** collaboration, co-ordination and information exchange between directorates and working/advisory groups to avoid silo working[199] and ensure coherence of institutional reforms and action plans.

- **Boost** the number of opportunities available for international or national external advisers to work co-located (if feasible) with the MoIA and the ANP, to provide mentoring and build staff capacity.

---

[198] The MoIA human resources plan

[199] Silo working occurs when several departments or groups within that organisation do not share information or knowledge with other individuals they work with i.e. barriers that exist between departments within an organization, causing people who are supposed to be on the same team to work against one another, including unintentionally.

Communications strategies

- **Prioritize** civilian and community-oriented policing activities via official communications channels and strategic messaging of the ANP, and reduce the level of emphasis placed on paramilitary aspects.

- **Promote and reinforce** examples of good policing by men and women to change Afghan public perception of the police and increase trust and legitimacy.

- **Consolidate** the actions that constitutes good behaviour and practice in policing, including using official communications to present guidance of good behaviour towards women.

- **Ensure** that imagery of women police in communications and recruitment campaigns reflects their expressed career aspirations to carry out clerical work, help women and children, undertake body searches, act as victim of crime helpline assistants, raise awareness about women's rights, or pursue justice for female victims and socially vulnerable groups.

- **Develop** public outreach campaigns in collaboration with religious and community leaders to change harmful public perceptions of women in the security sector.

Technical and operational-level recommendations

Gender and policing analysis

- **Conduct** institutional capacity and development assessments against *tashkeel* positions using a gender equity lens.

- **Undertake** periodic consultations and surveys to determine[200] women's preferred roles, working conditions and aspirations. Map changes in women's experiences and perceptions and make informed adjustments that respond to their recruitment, deployment, promotion and support needs. Given the rapidly changing security environment, it is particularly important to undertake a mapping exercise of this type.

- **Improve** the records and respective reasons of women officers who have resigned or failed to return to work, to identify the underlying reasons for attrition among women staff and inform the enaction of corresponding mitigation strategies.

- **Produce** in-depth analysis of security, ethnic, economic, religious and variations in gender norms and practices across provinces and districts, to identify those areas which should receive direct attention for sustainable advances in women's recruitment and deployment.

- **Consult** women police in the ANP and the MoIA, and women in other governmental departments and organizations regarding who they see as role models (and the reasons given for this), to help promote case studies of women in leadership.

Recruitment, training and deployment of women police

- **Adopt** inclusive, multi-entry pathways for women police which account for their diverse aspirations, using a mix of integrated, specialized, segregated and confined recruitment, training and deployment approaches.

---

[200] Research in other traditional and Islamic societies shows that while women often prefer to start off in gendered roles, as they grow in confidence (and as societal attitudes change), they are often likely to favour expanded work functions that include more mainstream roles. The pace of this change is slow, but women should not be constrained to gendered roles if they do not want to be. Qualitative (consultations) and quantitative (surveys) data collection measures could be used to track this dynamic.

- **Focus,** in the short-term, on growth and retention of women police in areas where they have made inroads, and where support networks and structures already exist, to solidify these gains.

- **Provide** funding for women police to participate in peer networking, e.g., International Association of Women Police training conferences and local and regional women police networks.

- **Hold** trainings for women police on building confidence to chair or participate in meetings that require facilitation, agenda setting and minute-taking skills. This could be achieved through funding women police to participate in training in conjunction with women working in health and social services or not-for-profit organizations, to develop skills on partnership policing and collaborative work.

Training (general)

- Expand gender sensitisation training for all police officers (especially men) to reduce the impact of harmful social norms, developed specifically for the Afghan context using narrative and interactive adult learning methods, including via mixed (police-community-multi-stakeholder) workshops.[201]

---

[201] Caparini, "Gender Training".

Bibliography

AIHRC. Situation of Women Employed in Defense and Security Sectors. Autumn 2017.

Amin, S. N. and Alizada, N. "Alternative Forms of Resistance: Afghan Women Negotiating for Change". Journal of International Women's Studies 21, 6 (2020): 361–78.

APPRO. Women in Afghan National Police: A Baseline Assessment. 2014.

Asia Foundation, The. A Survey of the Afghan People: Afghanistan in 2019.

Billing, L. "A Day on the Job With Kabul's Crime Scene Investigators". Aljazeera. February 1, 2021. *www.aljazeera.com/features/2021/2/1/in-afghanistan-a-day-on-the-job-with-kabuls-crime-scene-investi*

Brown, J. "European Policewomen: A Comparative Research Perspective". International Journal of Sociology of Law 25 (1997): 1–19.

Cahalan, L., Gitter, S. R., and Fletcher, E. K. "Terrorism and Women's Employment in Afghanistan". Oxford Development Studies 48, 2 (2020): 195–208. doi:10.1080/13600818.2020.1760813

Cao, L., Huang, L., and Sun, I.Y. Policing in Taiwan: From Authoritarianism to Democracy. Routledge, 2014.

Caparini, M. "Gender Training for Police Peacekeepers: Where Are We Now?" In Gender Roles in Peace and Security, edited by M. Scheuermann and A Zürn. Springer International, 2020.

Carrington, K., Guala, N., Puyol, M. V., and Sozzo, M. "How Women's Police Stations Empower Women, Widen Access to Justice and Prevent Gender Violence". International Journal for Crime, Justice and Social Democracy 9, 1 (2020).

Central Statistics Organisation. Afghanistan Living Conditions Survey 2016–17. Kabul: GIRoA, CSO, 2018.

Chan, J., Doran, S., and Marel, C. "Doing and Undoing Gender in Policing". Theoretical Criminology 14, 4 (2010): 425–46. doi:10.1177/1362480610376408.

Chu, D., and Abdulla, M. "Self-efficacy Beliefs and Preferred Gender Role in Policing: An Examination of Policewomen's Perceptions in Dubai, the United Arab Emirates". British Journal of Criminology 54, 3 (2014): 449–68.

Connell, R. "Accountable Conduct: 'Doing Gender' in Transsexual and Political Retrospect". Gender & Society 23, 1 (February 2009): 104–11. *https://doi.org/10.1177/0891243208327175*

Coyne, A. H. and Nyborg, I. "Pushing on a string? An Argument for Civil Society-driven Community Policing as Alternative to Ministry-centric Approach in Conflict-affected States". Journal of Human Security 16, 2 (2020): 31–43.

Denney, L. Policing and Gender. Geneva: Geneva Centre for Security Sector Governance (DCAF), 2019.

Desai, I., and Li, L. "Analyzing Female Labor Force Participation in Afghanistan: Identifying the Key Barriers that Prevent Women from Entering the Labor Force". Women's Policy Journal (2016).

Elizabeth Broderick & Co. Cultural Change: Gender Diversity and Inclusion in the Australian Federal Police. 2016. *www.afp.gov.au/culturalchange*

EU Annual Action Programme 2018 Part 2, 2019 Part 1 and 2020 Part 1 in Favour of Afghanistan to Be Financed from the General Budget of the Union. Ref. Ares (2018) 3231251 – 19/06/2018.

European Security and Defence College. Civilian Coordinator for Training in Security Sector Reform: ESDC EAB SSR Report on Training Requirements Analysis for Civilian CSDP Missions. 2020.

Friesendorf, C. "Insurgency and Civilian Policing: Organizational Culture and German Police Assistance in Afghanistan". Contemporary Security Policy 34, 2 (2013): 324–49. doi: *10.1080/13523260.2013.806186*

Fullerton, J. "Thai Police Academy Bans Women from Enrolling". The Guardian. September 5, 2018. *www.theguardian.com/world/2018/sep/05/thai-police-academy-bans-women-from-enrolling*

Garcia, V. Women in Policing Around the World: Doing Gender and Policing in a Gendered Organization. New York: Routledge, 2021.

Gordon, E., McHugh, C., and Townsley, J. "Risk versus Transformational Opportunities in Gender-Responsive Security Sector Reform". Journal of Global Security Studies (June 2020). *https://doi.org/10.1093/jogss/ogaa028*

Harsono, I. "The Development of Women and Children Service Unit within the Police – the Indonesian Experience". Presentation, 2nd International Islamic Women's Conference, Islamabad, Pakistan, November 21–24, 2011. *https://www.slideserve.com/jag/dr-i-rawati-h-arsono.*

Herrington, V., and Roberts, K. A. "Policing in Complexity: Leadership Lessons from an Annus Horribilis". Police Chief Online, February 10, 2021.

Human Rights Watch. "Afghanistan: Little Help for Conflict-Linked Trauma". October 7, 2019. *www.hrw.org/news/2019/10/07/afghanistan-little-help-conflict-linked-trauma*

Institute for Public Security of Catalonia. Women in Police Services in the EU: Facts and Figures 2012. February 2013. *www.recercat.cat/bitstream/handle/2072/207935/WOMEN%20IN%20POLICE%20SERVICES%20EU_2012.pdf*

INTERPOL, UN Women and UNODC. Women in Law Enforcement in the ASEAN Region. 2020.

Iskra, D., Trainor, S., Leithauser, M., and Segal, M. W. Women's Participation in Armed Forces Cross-Nationally: Expanding Segal's Model. Current Sociology 50, 5 (2002): 771–97. *https://doi.org/10.1177/0011392102050005009*

JICA and GIWPS. Case study on Afghanistan: Strengthening the Afghan National Police: Recruitment & Retention of Women Officers. Japan International Cooperation Agency and Georgetown Institute for Women, Peace and Security, 2016.

Kim, B., and Gerber, J. "Attitudes Toward Gender Integration in Policing: A Study of Police Cadets in China". International Journal of Law Crime and Justice 57 (2019): 91–102.

MacIntyre, K. "Rapid Assessment and Sample Surveys: Trade-offs in Precision and Cost". Health Policy and Planning 14, (1999): 363–73.

Marks, M. Transforming the Robocops: Changing Police in South Africa. Scottsville, South Africa: University of KwaZulu-Natal Press, 2005.

Ministry of Interior Affairs. Empowering the Women in Police: From Words to Action Roadmap 2021–2024. Afghanistan: MoIA, 2020.

Ministry of Interior Affairs. "First National Police-e-Mardume Conference: Summary of Proceedings". Kabul, Afghanistan: June 25, 2013. *https://ipcb. files.wordpress.com/2013/08/eupol-community-policing-report-july-20131.pdf*

Ministry of Interior Affairs. Incentives Code. MoIA, General Directorate of Police Law and Human, Child and Women's Rights Directorate, 2018.

Ministry of Interior Affairs. Incentives Code. MoIA, General Directorate of Police Law and Human, Child and Women's Rights Directorate, 2021.

Ministry of Interior Affairs. "Ten-Year Vision for the Afghan National Police: [2013–2023]". *https://moi.gov.af/en/vision-mission-0*

Ministry of Justice, "Police Law", Official Gazette No. 862, Kabul, September 22, 2005. *https://www.policinglaw.info/assets/downloads/2005_Police_Law_ of_Afghanistan.pdf*

Ministry of Public Health. National Mental Health Strategy 2019-2023. Afghanistan.

Murray, T. "Police-building in Afghanistan: A Case Study of Civil Security Reform". International Peacekeeping 14, 1 (2007): 108–26. doi:10.1080/13533310601114327

Murray, T. Report on the Status of Women in the Afghan National Police. Canadian International Development Agency, 2005.

Murray, T. Review of Women Policing Across the Globe: Shared Challenges and Successes in the Integration of Women Police Worldwide, by C. Rabe-Hemp and V. Garcia. Police Practice and Research 21, 5 (2020): 543–44. *https://doi.org/10.1080/15614263.2020.1765118.*

Natarajan, M. "Domestic Violence, Culture and Justice for Women". In Family Conversations: Let's Tell the Secrets, edited by E. R. Rocha. Addis Ababa, Ethiopia: Henrich Boll Foundation, 2007.

Natarajan, M. "Gender Equality in Law Enforcement: Make it real through Mentoring the Next Generation". Paper presented at International Association of Women Police Training Conference, Anchorage, Alaska, September 22–27, 2019.

Natarajan, M. "Police Culture and the Integration of Woman Officers in India". International Journal of Police Science and Management 16, 2 (2014): 124–39.

Natarajan, M. "Rapid Assessment of 'Eve Teasing' (Sexual Harassment) of Young Women During the Commute to College In India". Crime Science 5, 6 (2016). *https://doi.org/10.1186/s40163-016-0054-9.*

Natarajan, M. Women Police in a Changing Society: Back Door to Equality. Aldershot, UK: Ashgate, 2008.

Natarajan, M. "Women Police in a Traditional Society: Test of a Western Model of Integration". International Journal of Comparative Sociology 42, 1-2 (2001): 211–33. *https://doi.org/10.1163/156851801300171760*

Natarajan, M. "Women Police Units in India: A New Direction", Police Studies 19, 2 (1996): 63–76.

Natarajan, M., and Babu, D. "Women Police Stations: Have They Fulfilled Their Promise?" Police Practice and Research 21, 5 (2020): 442-58. doi:10. 1080/15614263.2020.1809827

Oxfam. "Women and the Afghan Police". Briefing paper. September 10, 2013.

Pervin, S. "Women in Leadership in the Police Administration of Bangladesh: A Review". Paper presented at the 6th International Law Enforcement and Public Health Conference, 2021.

Parlaktuna, İnci, and Sediqi, S. "The Effect of Socio-Cultural Norms on Female Labor Force Participation in Afghanistan". Kadın/Woman 2000, Journal for Women's Studies 21, 2 (2020): 19–41. *https://doi.org/10.33831/jws.v21i2.154*

Planty, D. J. and Perito, R. M. Police Transition in Afghanistan. Special Report 322. United States Institute of Peace, 2013.

Rabe-Hemp, C., and Garcia, V., eds. Women Policing across the Globe: Shared Challenges and Successes in the Integration of Women Police Worldwide. Rowman & Littlefield, 2020.

RUSI and FPRI. Reforming the Afghan National Police. Royal United Services Institute for Defence and Security Studies (London) and the Foreign Policy Research Institute (Philadelphia), 2009.

Safi, S. "Why Female Suicide in Afghanistan Is So Prevalent". BBC. July 1, 2018. *www.bbc.com/news/world-asia-44370711*

Segal, M. W. "Women's Military Roles Cross-Nationally: Past, Present, and Future", Gender and Society 9, 6 (1995): 757–75.

SIGAR. Support for Gender Equality: Lessons from the U.S. Experience in Afghanistan. Special Inspector General for Afghanistan Reconstruction, February 2021. *https://www.sigar.mil/pdf/lessonslearned/SIGAR-21-18-LL.pdf*

Singh, D. Investigating Corruption in the Afghan Police Force: Instability and Insecurity in Post-Conflict Societies. Bristol: Policy Press, 2020.

Sreekumaran Nair, N., Shrinivas Darak, Bhumika, T.V., Trupti Darak, Mathews, M., Ratheebhai, V., and Anjali Dave. "Gender-responsive Policing" Initiatives Designed to Enhance Confidence, Satisfaction in Policing Services and Reduce Risk of Violence Against Women in Low and Middle Income Countries – a Systematic Review: Implications of Evidence for South Asia. London: EPPI-Centre, Social Science Research Unit, UCL Institute of Education, University College London, December 2017.

Strobl, S. "Progressive or Neo-Traditional? Policewomen in Gulf Cooperation Council (GCC) Countries". Feminist Formations 22, 3 (2010): 51–74. *https://doi.org/10.1353/ff.2010.0028*

Strobl, S. "The Women's Police Directorate in Bahrain: An Ethnographic Exploration of Gender Segregation and the Likelihood of Future Integration". International Criminal Justice Review 18, 1 (2008): 39–58.

Strobl, S. "Towards a 'Women-Oriented' Approach to Post-Conflict Policing: Interpreting National Experience(s) and Intergovernmental Aspirations". International Journal for Crime, Justice and Social Democracy 9, 1 (2020): 95–111. *https://doi.org/10.5204/ijcjsd.v9i1.1465*

Suroush, Q. Assessing EUPOL Impact on Afghan Police Reform (2007–2016). Afghanistan Research and Evaluation Unit (EUNPACK), January 2018.

UNAMA. In Search of Justice for Crimes of Violence Against Women and Girls. UNAMA United Nations Office of the High Commissioner for Human Rights. December 2020.

UNDP. Afghanistan National Policewomen Census Survey. 2018.

UNDP. "Police Equipped to Combat COVID-19 Pandemic Effectively in Northern Provinces of Afghanistan". Accessed May 1, 2021. *www.af.undp.org/content/afghanistan/en/home/presscenter/pressreleases/2020/PoliceEquippedtoCombatCOVID-19inNorthernProvinces.html*

UNDP-LOTFA. Project document. Unpublished, 2015.

UNDP-LOTFA. Report on a Rapid Infrastructure Survey of Kabul City Police District Stations. Law and Order Trust Fund Afghanistan, 2019.

UNESCO. "UNESCO Stands with all Afghans to Ensure Youth and Adults in Afghanistan, Especially Women and Girls, Achieve Literacy and Numeracy by 2030". Press release, September 8, 2021. *https://en.unesco.org/news/unesco-stands-all-afghans-ensure-youth-and-adults-afghanistan-especially-women-and-girls*.

United Nations Population Fund. "Afghanistan's First Family Response Unit Open for Business". UNFPA, January 24, 2006. *www.unfpa.org/news/afghanistans-first-family-response-unit-open-business*

United Nations Population Fund. "Prosecuting Gender-based Violence in Afghanistan". UNFPA, February 17, 2016. *www.unfpa.org/news/prosecuting-gender-based-violence-afghanistan*

UNODC. "GLO.ACT Convenes 1st Meeting of its Women's Network Advisory Board". September 22, 2020. *www.unodc.org/unodc/en/human-trafficking/glo-act2/Countries/glo-act-convenes-1st-meeting-of-its-womens-network-advisory-board.html*

UNODC and GIRoA. Afghanistan Opium Survey 2019 – Socio-Economic Survey Report: Drivers, Causes and Consequences of Opium Poppy Cultivation. February 2021. *www.unodc.org/documents/crop-monitoring/Afghanistan/20210217_report_with_cover_for_web_small.pdf*

United Nations Security Council. S/RES/1325 (2000). Adopted October 31, 2000. *http://unscr.com/en/resolutions/doc/1325*

United Nations Security Council. S/RES/2151 (2014). Adopted 28 April, 2014. http://unscr.com/en/resolutions/2151

United Nations Security Council. Conflict-related Sexual Violence: Report of the Secretary-General. S/2021/312. United Nations, 2021. *https://undocs. org/S/2021/312*

UN Women and UNODC. Women in Law Enforcement in the ASEAN Region: Focus on Indonesia. Unpublished, 2021.

UN Women, UNODC and the International Association of Women Police. Handbook on Gender-responsive Police Services for Women and Girls Subject to Violence. 2021.

US Department of Defence. Enhancing Security and Stability in Afghanistan. December 2018. *https://media.defense.gov/2018/Dec/20/2002075158/-1/-1/1/1225-REPORT-DECEMBER-2018.PDF*

US Department of State and US Department of Defence. "Interagency Assessment of Afghanistan Police Training and Readiness". November 2006. *https://media.defense.gov/2006/Nov/01/2001713037/-1/-1/1/ Interagency%20Assessment%20of%20Afghanistan%20Police%20Training%20 and%20Readiness.pdf*

VEOHRC. Independent Review of Victoria Police. Victorian Equal Opportunity and Human Rights Commission. *https://www.humanrights. vic.gov.au/legal-and-policy/research-reviews-and-investigations/ police-review/*

WPSO and OXFAM. Afghan Women Police: Tomorrow's Force for Inclusive Security. Women & Peace Studies Organisation and OXFAM, July 2018. *https://wpso-afg.org/wp-content/uploads/2018/07/Afghan-Women-in-the-Police-Full-Report.pdf*

Williamson, M. "The Role of Women in Nation-Building: Rocking the Boat at the Risk of Making It Capsize?" Human Rights 13, 2 (2019): 85-112. *https://doi.org/10.22096/hr.2019.105277.1100.*

World Bank. "Labor Force Participation Rate, Female (% of Female Population Ages 15+) (Modeled ILO Estimate)". *https://data.worldbank.org/indicator/ SL.TLF.CACT.FE.ZS*

World Population Review. "Afghanistan Population 2019". *https:// worldpopulationreview.com/en/countries/afghanistan-population*

About the author

Melissa Jardine, PhD. is a former Australian police officer with a special interest in policing and security across the Asia region. She is a current member of the Strategic Planning Committee for the International Association of Women Police (IAWP). Her PhD explored police culture and socialisation and advocated for greater understanding of variations in policing, especially across the Global South. Dr Jardine has worked as a consultant and advisor for the United Nations, the International Criminal Police Organization (INTERPOL), the Global Law Enforcement and Public Health Association and is an Honorary Fellow at the Melbourne School of Population and Global Health at The University of Melbourne, Australia. In 2017, Dr Jardine was selected as an Asia 21 Young Leader by the Asia Society through a competitive process which identifies 'dynamic individuals who will impact global affairs over the coming decades'.

www.ingramcontent.com/pod-product-compliance
Lightning Source LLC
Chambersburg PA
CBHW071807090426
42737CB00012B/1988